T0300420

THE IMPACT OF CHINA'S ECONOMIC REFORMS UPON LAND, PROPERTY AND CONSTRUCTION

The Impact of China's Economic Reforms upon Land, Property and Construction

Edited by
JEAN JINGHAN CHEN
DAVID WILLS

Routledge
Taylor & Francis Group

LONDON AND NEW YORK

First published 1999 by Ashgate Publishing

Reissued 2018 by Routledge
2 Park Square, Milton Park, Abingdon, Oxon, OX14 4RN
711 Third Avenue, New York, NY 10017, USA

Routledge is an imprint of the Taylor & Francis Group, an informa business

Notice:
Product or corporate names may be trademarks or registered trademarks, and
are used only for identification and explanation without intent to infringe.

Publisher's Note
The publisher has gone to great lengths to ensure the quality of this reprint
but points out that some imperfections in the original copies may be
apparent.

Disclaimer
The publisher has made every effort to trace copyright holders and welcomes
correspondence from those they have been unable to contact.

A Library of Congress record exists under LC control number: 98073882

ISBN 13: 978-1-138-34366-5 (hbk)
ISBN 13: 978-0-429-43898-1 (ebk)

Contents

List of Figures

List of Tables

Map of China

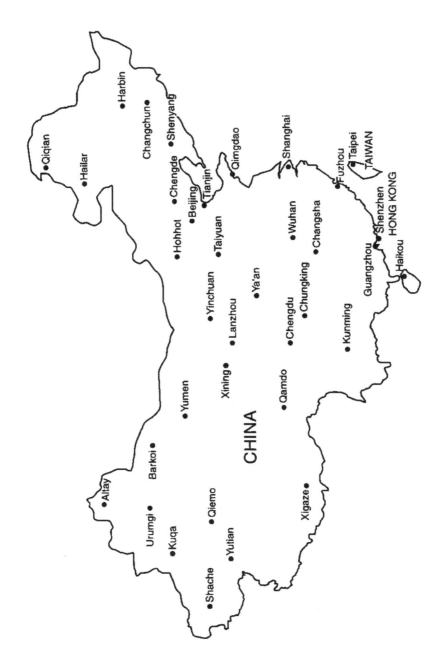

The Editors

Dr Jean Jinghan CHEN is Senior Research Fellow in the School of Land and Construction Management, Faculty of the Environment, the University of Greenwich. She obtained her Ph.D. in Economics at Lancaster University in 1992 and has been an active researcher and the author of more than 20 publications in the field of the Chinese Economy, Development Economics, Multinational Enterprises, Construction Economics and Management and Property Investment and Management. She has also engaged in consultancy work for major international donors and government agencies including the World Bank, the European Union, the Department for International Development and the Chinese Central and Provincial Governments.

Professor David Wills is the Dean of Faculty of the Environment and formerly the Director of Natural Resources Institute at the University of Greenwich. He is a fellow of the Royal Institution of Chartered Surveyors. He has written many articles in the field of Surveying, Construction Economics and Management. He first worked in China twenty years ago and, throughout the intervening years, has continued to work in several Chinese provinces and cities, and with many Chinese organisations and institutions. He has observed the economic transformation in China and seen the impact on the lives of many millions of people.

Preface

This book is the product of many years of experience in many people studying and working in China. Its prime objective is to explore the impact of China's recent economic reforms and dynamic economic progress on land use, the property market and construction activity.

The economic progress in China has occurred since the late 1970's under the leadership of DENG Xiaoping with his brand of 'authoritarian capitalism' or 'market Leninism'. This marked a shift from the doctrinaire centrally planned economy towards what DENG called a socialist market economy. 'What', as DENG once asked, 'does the colour of the cat matter as long as it catches mice?' Mice will continue to be caught even with DENG's death in February 1997. The reforms will continue to occur and economic progress will continue to be achieved, albeit with peaks and troughs on the way. The new government is in place and probably has been so for some years. It is probably true to say that real power passed from DENG long before his death. JIANG Zemin spent years consolidating his position and was confirmed as DENG's successor at the Party Congress in October 1997. The new government has confirmed continuation of DENG's philosophy. China is not going to fall apart because DENG is no longer its ultimate authority.

The economic and currency crises of the late 1990's in other countries in the region maybe pose a greater threat to China's economic stability than a change of leadership within. China's response to the regional economic problems is at present unclear (to devalue or not to devalue?). Thus, the effects of its response to these regional problems on its own economic progress and thus on further land reforms and the growing property markets and construction activity remain to be seen.

This book concentrates on the reforms and progress up to the time of DENG's death.

Acknowledgements

Over the past twenty years many organisations and institutions in China have assisted us in our work. The central government's State Land Administration in Beijing, and its provincial bureaux in Jilin, Sichuan and Zhejiang as well as the municipal bureaux in Changchun, Chengdu, Chongqing and Ningbo have all in recent years contributed substantially to our understanding of the impact of economic reform on the land, property and construction sectors. Mr Zou Yuchuan, the Director of the State Land Administration, and his colleagues always gave generously of their time.

Many other people supported and contributed to this book. They are: Professor David Chambers, Professor David Isaac, Dr Peter Glaves and Elias Arkoulis from the University of Greenwich; Dr LI Ling Hin, Keith McKinnell, Professor Anthony Walker and Dr Andrew Hamer from the University of Hong Kong; and LI Ling from the State Land Administration of the People's Republic of China. Individual chapters were drafted as follows:

Preface: David Wills

Chapter 1: Introduction, Jean Jinghan CHEN and David Wills

Chapter 2: Urban Land Management in China, Andrew Hamer

Chapter 3: Development of Urban Land Policies in China, LI Ling and David Isaac

Chapter 4: China's Land Reform and the Establishment of a Property Market, Keith McKinnell and Anthony Walker

Chapter 5: Pricing of Land in China's Reforms, LI Ling Hin

Chapter 6: The impact of Chinese Economic Reforms upon the Construction Industry, Jean Jinghan CHEN

Chapter 7: Foreign Investment in the Construction Industry, Jean Jinghan CHEN

Chapter 8: Social Cost-Benefit Analysis of China's Construction Investment, Jean Jinghan CHEN

Chapter 9: Pioneer Urban Housing Reform in China, Jean Jinghan CHEN and David Wills

Chapter 10: Sustainable Development, David Chambers, Jean Jinghan CHEN, Peter Glaves and Elias Arkoulis

1 Introduction

Asia Pacific

The dynamic growth of the Asia Pacific market economies is helping to shape contemporary geopolitics. This growth has evolved over decades. The current economic take-off of one quarter of the human race (China plus the littoral countries) is transforming the political and economic structure of the entire globe.

After the initial chaos that was Asia following the second world war, Japan grew to be a major industrial power and economic success story and came to dominate Asia Pacific. The late 1960's and 1970's saw a second wave of economic development which consolidated other areas of Asia Pacific - Singapore, South Korea, Hong Kong and Taiwan. The 1980's saw Malaysia, Thailand and Indonesia begin to flourish economically and China, seduced by the economic progress surrounding it, was drawn into the Western economic system. China has become the world's fastest growing economy. China's economic success has not been confined to raw economic growth. By 1992 foreign trade had risen to US $166 billion (ADB,1991), signifying that China had moved to being one of the world's major trading nations. An IMF study found that China's economy is presently the third biggest (after USA and Japan) in the world and would be the largest within a decade if the same pattern of growth is sustained (IMF,1993). This has greatly enhanced the weight of the Asia Pacific region in global politics and the global economy.

Japan's role in the economic development of Asia Pacific has been crucial, and the development in recent decades has been powered by Japan. However, it is China that is now providing and will continue to provide the thrust for an even more dynamic regional economy.

Despite the slow down that has occurred in the world economy in the early 1990's, the pace of economic development in Asia Pacific remained unabated until 1997. It has been the fastest growth region in the world. The average economic growth rate in Asia Pacific has been about three times the average growth rate in the developing world as a whole (IMF,1993).

1

The economic and currency crises of the late 1990's, which affected the Asia Pacific region, particularly Thailand, Malaysia and Indonesia, were brought about by a combination of overheating, over confidence, bad loans, poor risk assessment and a lack of probity in government. Undoubtedly, confidence in the region, and in the world about the region, has been damaged. A period of adjustment is required before there is a return to a generally upward economic trend. Crucial to re-establishing the stability and growth of recent decades is the reaction to these events by China and its new leaders.

A crucial factor triggering the high economic growth rates for Asia Pacific has been foreign direct investment (FDI). FDI is playing an increasing role in the world economy generally, and particularly in the Asia Pacific economies. The United Nations reported that the flow of world-wide FDI rose at an annual rate of almost 30% in the 5 years up to 1989 (UN,1991). This was three times as fast as the growth of trade generally. The total stock of foreign direct investment at the beginning of the 1990's rose to US $ 1.5 trillion.

FDI is increasingly important in economic development because of its close links with trade, financial flows and technology transfer. The Asia Pacific countries have particularly benefited from FDI. Relatively low labour costs and an open and receptive policy environment in the recipient countries have been the main lures for foreign capital flows, together with the move towards high technology and skill intensive industries. FDI has transformed the economies of the Asia Pacific region, and investment boomed as a result of the large number of foreign investment projects and the consequential increase in construction and public infrastructure projects.

The construction industry has played a leading role in the expanding economies of the Asia Pacific region, both benefiting from the developing commercial and industrial base and contributing to it, by attracting investment from countries both within the region and from outside it. Construction's percentage share of the gross domestic product varies from country to country in the region (for example about 5% in China and about 9% in Japan). Similarly the growth rate of each country's construction industry annually varies, but the growth has almost always been substantial in recent years until the crises of the late 1990's.

Dynamic economic growth has put enormous pressure on infrastructure, and vast sums must be spent to bring it up to adequate levels.

Most of the countries in the region launched very ambitious infrastructure development plans in the early 1990's to address these problems. The private sector too in Asia Pacific has spent, and will continue to spend, very large sums of money on commercial, residential, tourist and industrial related projects.

The primary growth sectors in the construction industry in Asia Pacific are energy, transport and environment. Asia Pacific is in the midst of an electricity crisis brought on by the booming growth and the profligate use of energy. Virtually every country in the region is facing a potential energy crunch. For example peninsula Malaysia regularly suffers isolated power cuts resulting in millions of dollars worth of lost production. Cheap, dependable electricity is vital for continued economic expansion. The amount of investment needed for new electricity production is huge. The World Bank expects that 14 Asian countries (excluding Japan) will spend almost US $500 billion on generation, transmission and distribution this decade. China will account for some 40-50% of this total according to the World Bank. About 60% of the new capacity in the developing world will be built in Asia Pacific countries.

With the rapid growth of vehicular traffic in the cities, the governments of the countries in Asia Pacific are progressively giving more emphasis to the development of subway and mass transit systems. Presently, only Japan (Tokyo, Osaka and Kyoto), have heavy rail mass transit systems. Taipei (Taiwan) Shanghai, Tianjin (PRC) and Seoul (South Korea) are currently building their subways, whilst Hong Kong and Singapore have recently extended their systems. Anyone who has travelled in the major cities of Asia Pacific will know of the serious traffic problems - mass transit systems are vital to avoid the cities' transport systems collapsing under the strain and grinding to a halt.

By the early part of the next decade, Bangkok will have its own mass transit railway system, as will Manila, Kuala Lumpur, and several cities in Taiwan and the PRC (Guangzhou, Qingdao, Nanjing, Shenyang, Dalian, Chongqing, Changchun and Harbin).

One of the largest projects in the Asia Pacific is the construction of the new airport and port development in Hong Kong. Although dogged in the early days by the unique political differences between UK, Hong Kong and China, the construction of the airport is nearly complete, and together with its associated infrastructure, will take until early in the 21st century to complete fully and will cost something like US$10 billion. Other airports in the region are being built at Bangkok, Kuala Lumpur, Seoul, two in Taiwan and two in Indonesia.

Major highways are being constructed throughout China; there are traffic alleviation schemes planned for 6 major cities in South Korea; a new expressway system in Singapore and a second stage in the development of the expressway in Bangkok is underway.

The rapid pace of industrialisation and urbanisation in Asia Pacific has introduced a new set of problems that most Asia Pacific countries are now struggling to handle; problems such as solid and liquid waste control noise and air pollution. The rises in waste generated has spurred Taiwan, South Korea and Hong Kong to spend record breaking sums on the construction of incineration plant, sewage systems and garbage processing plant.

Another economic sector that has grown dramatically in the last decade and will continue into the 21st century is tourism. Tourism has been a significant contribution to the region's construction boom. The Asia Pacific region has sustained tremendous growth over the last half of the 1990's. According to a report by the Economic Intelligence Unit, overall tourist arrivals in Asia Pacific will expand at an annual rate of 7% until the year 2000. This increasing demand spurs construction in hotels, resorts, entertainment centres and shopping complexes, in addition to the airports previously mentioned.

However, it is the growing importance of China's economic take off in the region, and in the world that will have the greatest effect and provide a massive construction market. The take off, which began with the implementation of DENG Xiaoping's economic reform plan in 1979 and is being carried through by JIANG Zemin and ZHU Rongji, is eliminating poverty at a prodigious rate, and has produced the world's fastest growing economy as China has become reintegrated with the world economy. China's economic boom is reshaping the economies of Asia Pacific. And economic progress requires effective land and property use and development through construction.

China's Economic Reform and Development

China is the world's biggest developing socialist country. The establishment of the People's Republic of China in 1949 by the Chinese Communist Party marked the liquidation of the semi-feudal heritage and brought a degree of unity and identity to China that had been missing for almost a century. The Long March generation of senior communists has played the major role in national politics ever since, and the history of the period since 1949 has to a large extent been of their personal battles for power, and for differing visions of socialism. The struggle was at its most intense during the Cultural Revolution of 1966-78. After the death of Mao in 1976, DENG Xiaoping controlled the country through a succession of younger men who shared his insistence on the importance of economic advance as opposed to political purity. In 1978, the economic reforms and the open door policy were announced, and the Cultural Revolution was reassessed as a 'national disaster'. The period has never been free of tensions between 'reformers' and 'conservatives' who worried about the dilution of socialist orthodoxy brought by greater economic liberalism. Market-oriented reforms and a rapid expansion of foreign trade brought demands for political changes, which the Communist Party has never been prepared to countenance and resulted in the 'Tiananmen Square Event' in 1989. The Event was followed by a period of intense political repression and an obsession with the need for 'stability'. The collapse of communism in the former Soviet Union, however, led to a rethink. It was argued that the main pressure on the leaders was not for democratisation but rather for achieving healthy economic growth. In 1992 the Communist Party launched a new campaign for faster and bolder economic reforms, endorsed by the Communist Party's 14th National Congress, held in October 1992. The stress in political rhetoric was no longer on the importance of Marxist orthodoxy, but on the need to achieve rapid economic growth by whatever means seemed most appropriate.

China's population of 1.2 billion is the largest in the world. Population density varies between the developed eastern coastal region, for example, 2159 per km^2 in Shanghai, and a mere 2 per km^2 in the remote western region. Well over 90% of the population live in the eastern third of the country. Vast areas of western China consist of either deserts or mountains. About 80% of the population still live in farming communities. Putonghua, based on the capital Beijing dialect, has become the official state language and is taught in all schools (SSBC,1993). By the end of 1993, living standards, measured in terms of annual income per capita, have improved greatly, reaching about US$280. Life expectancy at birth was 70 years. The number of illiterates and semi-illiterates (people 12 years of age and above who cannot read or can read only a few words) was 15% of the population. However, the percentage of the population having attained higher education is extraordinarily low. In 1993 only 2 million people were enrolled in higher education, less that 2% of the estimated 130 million people aged 20-24 (WB,1993).

China has been pursuing a centrally planned economy since 1949. For a long time China was reluctant to absorb ideas and products from abroad. During 1949-60 China accepted assistance only from the Soviet Union for instituting a centrally planned economy and establishing the industrial base and infrastructure of the country. Relations between China and the Soviet Union broke down in 1960 and the Soviet Union withdrew all loans and specialists and technical personnel from China. From 1967 to 1977 China was virtually isolated from the rest of the world. The programme of economic reforms announced in 1978 recognised that the modernisation of the country could only be achieved through co-operation with developed countries. Thus the 'door' admitting foreign trade and investment opened. In many respects China is trying to learn from the experience of the South East Asian countries, such as Hong Kong, Singapore, South Korea and Taiwan. Foreign investment is thus viewed as a major source of technology and an instrument of export promotion.

The setting up of the four Special Economic Zones (SEZs) in the southern coastal provinces in 1980 was a testimony to the open door policy. The SEZs, which resemble the export processing zones in other Asian countries, were designed to attract foreign investment. This was followed by the designation of the 14 coastal cities in 1984 and Hainan Island in 1988 (which was given provincial status and is the largest SEZ in China, perhaps in the world) as preferential sites for foreign direct investment (FDI). (In some ways, the establishment of the SEZs was a return to the concept of the foreign concessionary ports that flourished economically in the earlier part of the 20th century.) Meanwhile came the promulgation of the Joint Venture Law and other regulations concerning economic reforms, such as regulations on land use and the property market, which were designed to deregulate central government control, practise taxation reform, promote foreign trade and international co-operation and attract FDI in many fields by providing preferential treatment for them. These measures were aimed to build up a market economy (which in China is known as a 'market economy with Chinese characteristics') and provide an environment as similar as possible to Western countries for international corporations.

After the success of these economic reforms, particularly in Guangdong province, China is now opening virtually all of the country to the world. The Pudong economic zone in Shanghai, for example, has aroused widespread interest. Under the plan towards the year 2000, the country has been divided into three areas for the purpose of development priorities. The eastern seaboard is to concentrate on the absorption of advanced technology and serve as the conduit for the introduction of new technology in general. The central region, where the majority of energy and mineral resources are concentrated, is to give priority to their development. In the poorest western region, agriculture and animal husbandry are to be emphasised.

China has been developing at an amazing speed since 1980. Gross domestic product (GDP) climbed by an impressive yearly average of 9.4% in real terms during 1980-91 and 12.8% during 1992-1994. The gross value of industrial output grew by an average annual rate of 17% during 1980-91, and about 27% during 1992-93, with a share of 57% in GDP in 1991.

The average annual growth rate of agricultural output was 6% during 1980-90 and 4% during 1991-93, with a share of 27% of GDP in 1991. The share of services in GDP grew from 23% in 1980 to 27% in 1993. Fixed investment grew at an average annual rate of 13% during 1980-91 and 23.3% during 1992-94, with a share in GDP of 32% in 1992. National income grew at an average annual rate of 8% during 1980-91 and around 12% during 1992-94. The total value of exports and imports in 1994 were US$121 billion and US$115.9 billion respectively, with a trade surplus of US$5.1 billion. Foreign exchange reserves were US$51.6 billion by the end of 1994 (WB,1993,1994,1995) (EIU,1994,1995) (SSBC,1993,1994,1995). Table 1.1 summarises the major economic statistics in China during the period 1988 to 1996.

About this Book

The rapid economic reform has had a great influence on the land, property and construction sectors. Land, property and construction reform have played a very important role in the entire economic reform and have collectively become one of the driving forces of the national economy. There can be no economic development without land use and construction activity. This book studies the impact of the economic reforms upon some aspects of land, property and construction and their influence in the national economy. Further, it provides a view on how management of the physical environment needs to be considered in the context of economic progress to achieve sustainable development.

Chapter 2 summarises the joint study, which was made by the World Bank and China's State Land Administration Bureau at the beginning of the

Table 1.1   China: Main Economic Indicators, 1988-1996

	1988	1989	1990	1991	1992	1993	1994	1995	1996
GNP (Rmb bn; current prices)	1 406	1 601	1 768	2 022	2 402	3 137	4 113e	4 523e	5 411
Real GNP growth (%)	11.3	4.3	4.0	7.7	13.0	13.4	12	8.8e	8.6e
GNP per head (Rmb bn; current prices)	1 280	1 433	1 549	1 756	2 061	2 661	3 439e	3 732e	4 399
Population (bn)	1.1	1.12	1.14	1.15	1.16	1.18	1.20	1.21e	1.23e
Labour force (m)	--	553.3	567.4	583.6	594.3	602.2	--	--	--
Gross fixed asset investment (Rmb bn; current prices)	449.7	413.8	444.9	550.9	785.5	1 245.8	1 593.0	1 800e	2 160e
Real change of gross fixed asset investment (%)	15.5	0.2	-1.3	6.5	25.0	27.0	18.0	16.0e	12.5e
National income (Rmb bn; current prices)	1 173.8	1 317.6	1438.4	1 655.7	2 022.3	2 488.2	3 235e	4 205e	5 467e
National income per head (Rmb bn; current prices)	1 066	1 178	1 267	1 439	1 736	2 111	2 696e	3 475e	4 445e
Inflation (%) Urban consume prices	20.7	16.3	1.3	5.1	8.6	19.6	25e	13.9e	12e
Industrial production	16.5	14.5	2.0	3.0	4.0	12.0	17.0e	18.2e	--
Interest rate on loans (%)	8.3	11.2	10.1	9.0	9.0	9.8	11.0e	15.0e	15.0e
Exchange rate (Rmb:$)	3.72	3.77	4.78	5.32	5.51	5.76	8.68	8.30e	9.50e
Merchandise exports ($ bn)	41.1	43.2	51.5	58.9	69.6	75.7	121.0	113.9e	127.6e
Real change of exports (%)	8.1	-1.8	17.7	16.9	15.8	11.1	31.9	10.1e	6.8e
Merchandise imports ($ bn)	-46.4	48.8	-42.4	-50.2	-64.4	-86.3	-115.9	-113.9e	-125.3e
Real change of imports (%)	0.3	-10.7	0.4	20.4	24.6	30.9	11.2	17.5e	4.7e
Trade balance ($ bn)	-5.3	-5.6	9.2	8.7	5.2	-10.6	5.1	19.3e	2.3e
Current-account balance ($ bn)	-3.8	-4.3	12.0	13.2	6.4	-11.8	7.7	-1.0e	1.3e
Total debt (incl undisbursed) ($ bn)	40.0	44.8	52.5	60.8	68.3	77.0	87.0e	94.0e	101.0e
Reserves (incl gold) ($ bn)	--	18.0	29.6	43.7	20.6	20.8	51.6	61.4e	--
FDI utilised ($ bn)	2.2	2.6	2.6	3.3	7.3	23	--	--	--

e: EIU estimates.

Sources : [EIU, 94, 95] [SSCB, 93, 94, 95].

1990s, on urban land management issues and options for China. Several suggestions are raised regarding the key issue of how to bring the land reform process to a successful conclusion.

Chapter 3 reviews urban land policy in China and provides the historical background of urban land development. The chapter further investigates recent legislation and looks at proposals for the future.

Chapter 4 examines the political and economic evolution of land use rights in China. From this basis it reviews the current state of the market in property and points out the major problems which China faces in developing a mature market and the prospects for the emergence of such a market. A focus is also provided on the most active region - the Pearl River Delta - and the influence of Hong Kong on both the reforms and the market.

Chapter 5 discusses the attempts by the Chinese authorities to develop a guideline land price system at the beginning of the land use rights reforms to reflect the official view of the pricing of land. An examination of this official view of land price may explain some of the reasons for the specific land price behaviour resulting from the privatisation of land use rights in China.

Chapter 6 assesses the impact of economic reforms upon the construction industry by studying constraints on economic growth, construction and investment and construction and the national economy. It also investigates the type of construction companies and points out the problems inherent in the construction industry.

Chapter 7 shows that the heavy demand for construction caused by rapid economic growth cannot be satisfied by China's prevailing resources. This huge emerging construction market has attracted world-wide interest. The Chapter explores the consequent opportunities for foreign construction companies and analyses the foreign participants and the problems they have encountered in the Chinese market. Some recommendations for future co-operation between Chinese and foreign contractors are put forward.

Chapter 8 analyses public construction investment made by the Chinese government by using a cost-benefit technique to build up a social cost-benefit model. The Chinese government has made substantial construction investment to establish the Special Economic Zones to attract foreign direct investment, which has been viewed as a major source of technology and an instrument of export promotion. It is, therefore, of interest to examine the extent to which the construction investment benefits society.

The chapter answers the question that to what extent the contribution of this investment to national economic welfare justifies the expenditure.

Chapter 9 studies the policies and performance of urban housing reform in China. Housing provision in urban areas has been a major social and economic issue. The major housing problem in China is the scarcity of housing supply. The chapter analyses the initial housing reform prior to 1993 and points out the reasons for the lack of success and the lessons drawn from it. The chapter also studies the present reform program from 1993 and highlights the problems associated with it.

Finally, Chapter 10 provides a perspective on environmental land management and considers the relationships between sustainable development, land use planning and environmental planning and their value as a policy tool. Environmental land management has an important function to play in China's developing economy. The chapter considers the significance of China as a developing economy and its actual and potential environmental impact at a national and international level and justifies the validity of evaluating China's Agenda 21 at this stage in its development. The chapter also provides an outline of British experience in its formulation and implementation of Agenda 21 and explores it as a possible framework for application in the context of a developing economy like China. This concluding chapter makes recommendations for changes in policy and practice, which are necessary if sustainable development is to become a Chinese and global reality rather than merely a vision.

2 Urban Land Management in China: Completing the Policy Agenda

At the beginning of the decade, the World Bank and China's State Land Administration jointly conducted a study on urban land management issues and options for China. That report focused on several themes, and in retrospect the key outstanding issue is how to bring the reform process to a successful conclusion (WB,1992).

That report was deliberately far-ranging in nature. In particular, attention was paid to:

- Price and Property rights
- Urban planning
- Resource mobilisation; and
- Information processing

Much has been accomplished, yet more remains to be done. The criteria for judging future success are now encapsulated by two objectives: preserving arable land at the urban periphery, while completing property rights reforms in urban areas. The other objectives are sub-ordinate to these two.

Arable Land

The issue of preserving arable land has become clearer after examining the problem from both the perspective of the cities that supervise each local metropolitan region and that of local authorities in the metropolitan periphery who make day-to-day decisions. Essentially, rural land available for conversion to urban use is severely under-taxed, given the importance assigned by the State to its preservation. Expected profits from conversion are perceived as very high, as local officials plan for economic and technology zones in the absence of feasibility studies; while accommodating future residential and employment growth in the town proper.

At this stage, it appears that one way to resolve this problem is to re-centralise the required permission process to an administrative level high enough to carefully consider all consequences. Alternatively, conversion fees payable to the State should be drastically increased.

Town Planning

Town suffer from inadequate supervision, while appearing to have little autonomy one case in point is the cited arable land issue, a second involves urban planning, while some coastal towns have adopted minimum development density controls, many others appear to believe that prosperity depends on providing outsiders with cheap land and few density restrictions. Because few local urban planners exist (or local government officials, for that matter), this open-ended, unsupervised approach threatens to make a mockery of Government objectives. Even if higher-level jurisdictions are mobilised to deal with the arable land issue, the mossy details involving individual urban planning permits can only be granted (and thus decided) locally.

Unfortunately, the consequences of poor local planing do not stop at the misuse of arable land for urban purposes. It is at the sub-metropolitan, town and township level that one can appreciate the enormous damage done by inadequate environmental management. Due to a lack of sensitivity to the environment, China's countryside is being poisoned by a thoughtless attack on air and water resources. Those charged with protecting the environment have little power and limited funds with which to control the damage done. As a result, solid and liquid wastes are often discarded in a hazardous manner; even toxic wastes may be disposed of in ways that guarantee future problems. In this and other instances, one must be reminded that reform does not necessarily mean less government, but a redirected effort to achieve very precise objectives.

Towns as Pioneers

This focus on is justified for reasons other than those already cited. Today, taking into account residents with permanent status to live in urban areas, as well as those longer-term residents granted only 'temporary' residency status, the towns of China hold one-third of the country's actual 400 million urban population. Within 15-20 years, that total will double to 800 million, and much of that urbanisation will take place at the periphery of existing urban areas, in today's towns but tomorrow's cities. Managing that growth will be as critical as any policy measure taken since 1979, when the process of modernisation through reform began.

For that reason, it is imperative that towns complete the price and property rights reforms within the shortest possible time frame. Then, once again, the countryside can surround the cities, this time by the power of example. Given the small size of towns (often only 2 or 3 square kilometres) it is important that: newly urbanised land be provided in the form of leaseholds, at price set competitively, and land allocated through administrative means be converted to leasehold status within a certain time. In the latter case, this means immediately charging users the annual rent equivalent of a market value lease. Within a few years, the users would have to obtain a lease or sell their de facto ownership rights, vacate the land, and retain a percentage of the relevant revenues, as provided by law. The only exceptions should be established for non-profit uses; including schools, hospitals, and administrative or military facilities.

The City Agenda

All city land be it newly-urbanised, redeveloped, or claimed by existing users, should be forced to the discipline of the market.

For the first two categories cited, newly-urbanised land should never be granted on concessionaire or non-competitive terms except for rare instances when it can be justified. Redevelopment, by definition, replaces old users with new ones, and even grants old users revenues with which to pay for a land lease elsewhere. Once again, new users should not be granted quasi-ownership rights unless they can afford to pay for the privilege.

The greatest obstacle to introducing market mechanism lies in finding a way to convert the land holding of existing users provided with administratively allocated land. In turn, the vested interests of two powerful groups are affected: 'public housing' tenants as well as State-owned enterprise managers and workers. This obstacle is far more serious in cities than in towns where individual initiative is more pronounced. Nevertheless the solution proposed for town users of administratively allocated land still has merit. A form of leasehold could be developed which is payable either as a lump sum or an annual rent equivalent, with rent calculated as 'interest' earned by the notional value of the lease. Over a longer period than allowed in towns, cities would transform such leaseholds into the conventional kind already in place.

However, to ease the burden of buying a lease, leases would be allowed to pay in instalments lasting several years. A practice already adopted by Shenzhen.

Public housing rent reform program needs to be accelerated, so that by the year 2000, average rents can reach a level three or four times the current level of approximately one Renminbi Yuan per occupied square meter. Prices charged under home ownership schemes can then also begin to rise. Given the speed with which average household incomes are increasing, this should not create a serious affordability problem. The inability of particular types of tenants to pay for this price reform should be tackled directly by developing appropriate income supplement solutions. Under no circumstances should the problem of a minority slow down the reform. Once housing reforms are accelerated, land lease solutions can be gradually introduced. Furthermore, what applies to tenants should also apply to homeowners with affected workers and employers sharing the cost burden.

Enterprises must also anticipate. The overall reform process will gradually resolve the issue of loss-making enterprises. One must begin to plan for a day (in the not too distant future) when all enterprises are run in a business-like manner. Chronic loss-makers will (in one way or another) be disbanded and their assets recycled to better uses. Once this begins to happen the proposed property rights reform should follow. More profitable housing businesses should begin the transition earlier.

Land, Buildings and Resource Mobilisation

Local government finances need to be restructured. At present too high a proportion of property related revenues are linked to the rural-urban land conversion process. In turn, this creates perverse invectives to accelerate the process of urbanising rural land. Therefore, it is now important to take additional measures. First, as already suggested, local government profits from conversion should be subject to very careful reporting to higher level authorities and also taxed more heavily. Second, occupants of previously developed land must pay for the privilege in two ways: (a) by obtaining leaseholds, as already suggested; and (b) by paying some form of annual property tax. The second proposal requires elaboration. A one-time payment for the right to lease land can be justified for many reasons, including the need to help finance the major infrastructure public works that make a town or city viable. However, every local administration incurs annual expenses inked to providing services to property owners and tenants; services as varied as education, law and order, and fire prevention. For various reasons, alternative ways of financing these activities are inadequate (either because of tax evasion or central control of the relevant revenues). While planning a major expansion of leasehold coverage in existing 'built up' areas, local authorities should impose annual taxes on property 'owners'. This will have the indirect effect of reducing incentives to generate needed revenue by converting rural land to urban uses.

Concluding Thoughts

Much time could be spent on advocacy of reforms that speed up the introduction of modern management tools. While cities, taken as a whole, have clearly begun the process of overhauling the way information is gathered, processed, and utilised, towns appear generally quite unprepared. Field visits to towns across various provinces suggest local governments are undermanned, drastically short of equipment, and forced to work with outdated information. Offices housing critical local organs often have little but four walls, desks, chairs and the odd abacus plus filing cabinet. A concerted, national effort to learn from best practices across China is long overdue.

The cited World Bank report urged state authorities to establish a Leading Group on Urbanisation, thus forcing otherwise independent minded Ministries and Commissions to work together. Unfortunately, to date the advice has been adopted only partially through the creation of a Leading Group off Town Development. Though welcome, more is needed. China's urbanisation has been long since ceased to be a matter of improving the management of individual centres, though both cities and towns could benefit from initiatives that merely improved local administration. Today, however, vast metropolitan regions are becoming a characteristic of Chinese urbanisation, just as is the case around the world. Interdependence is the critical byword as a result, cross-boundary issues have emerged as critical, and ignored variables. Cities are expanding into the countryside; and an urbanising countryside is moving towards the cities. If this cross-administration issue is ignored, then State goals concerning arable land and sustainable development will remain unfulfilled. All responsible agencies most sit around the same table and assume their share of responsibility. The greatest rural-urban transition in world history requires nothing less.

3 Development of Urban Land Policies in China

This chapter looks at urban land policy in China and is in three sections: the historical background; recent legislation and proposals for the future.

Historical Background

The ownership of land in China is basically of two types. Firstly, there is state-owned land mainly in cities and towns although the state also owns large forests and some farm land. The second type of land ownership is that owned by rural collectives which is land in rural areas and sometimes in towns not owned by the state.

The state owned land system has been established in a series of distinct phases since 1945. Between 1945 and 1949, the Chinese Communist Government nationalised land owned by the Nationalist Government. In this phase, land was also recovered from landowners who had supported the nationalists. From 1949, the Chinese government and its associated administration and organisations obtained land by buying and renting at market levels from private land owners and this continued until 1953. On the 5 December 1953, the State Council of the People's Republic of China passed laws, which provided for the requisitioning of land for state construction purposes. Under these laws, all government organisations and state owned enterprises were provided with land, which was requisitioned by the government. The land then became state owned and returned to the state when the use finished. However, during the period from 1949 to 1956, private land continued to exist and could be sold, leased and given away. From 1956 onward, the government of the People's Republic of China proceeded to complete the nationalisation of land, a process which was completed around 1982. On the 4 December 1982, the 5th session of the National People's Congress passed the *Constitution of the People's Republic of China.* Clause 4 article 10 of the Constitution stipulated:

'No organisation or individual may appropriate, buy, sell or lease or unlawfully transfer land in other ways'.

Thus, until recently, the land system which was established has meant that urban land was owned by the state, land being allocated by the state to users without charge or limitation on the length of use and any private land transaction was prohibited. This system of land allocation is now referred to as the 'old land system' or 'old land use system'. The old land system was basically a product of China's economy during this period.

Until the end of the 1970s the economy was a planned economy, there was a planned allocation of resources so markets in factors of production did not exist. There were only two types of economic enterprise, state owned and collective owned enterprises. The financial interests of the managers and workers in the enterprises were divorced from the performance of the enterprise. There was no incentive to compete with other enterprises. Factors of production including land, raw materials, machinery were allocated by government. The prices of these factors were fixed by the state as accounting measures and did not bear any relationship to market price, there were no private property rights. Managers and workers in state-owned enterprises lived in the houses provided by the enterprise. Some had private houses, but with no land attached and no transfer of ownership of these houses was allowed. The state owned enterprises and collectives basically continued the production of the same type of goods for which they had been established and losses were subsidised by the state. There was no need to maximise the efficient use of the factors of production under this economy and under these circumstances a land market was considered irrelevant and the private market would 'wither away'.

Recent Legislation

From 1979 on, the Chinese government began to institute policies of economic reform, its 'open-door' policies which have included reforms in agrarian production, foreign capital investment, incentives for production, reforms of the financial system and the introduction of free markets. In detail, these have consisted of:

- *Rural production reform.* Since 1979, the government began to popularise the rural contractual system which delegated the responsibility for determining output to producers. This resulted in a higher crop yield and in a crop surplus. Because of the increase in production and productivity less workers were required on the land and this has released surplus manpower who have moved into urban areas to find work or set up township enterprises in the countryside.

- Also from 1979 on, the government began to establish *foreign investment ventures*, either equity joint ventures, co-operative ventures and wholly foreign owned ventures.
- The parallel of the system to establish responsibility for agrarian production is a similar system applied to *urban indigenous enterprises*, these enterprises now have an incentive-based system which has also allowed the establishment of individual property rights.
- There has been reform of the *financial system* instead of profits being taken by local and central government, a tax is now levied on the profit and this tax is shared between local and central government.
- There has been reform of the *price system*, central government price control on commodities and raw materials has lessened and the price determined in the markets has now become the important factor in the distribution of goods and raw materials.

A new economic system has now been established and is referred to as a 'socialist market economy' and differs from the previous planned economy in a number of critical aspects. In the market-driven economy, incentive-based competition between enterprises has arisen and managers and workers now have interests and returns more closely allied to profitability. The 'old land system' is now inappropriate for the changes which have taken place in the economy, this system now needs to change particularly because the lack of a land market is depriving both central and local government of the chance of raising finance through land sales for infrastructure development in urban areas. The lack of a land market leads to an inefficient allocation of land resources and lack of flexibility in the relocation of business uses. The 'old land system' does not attract foreign investment as there are no clear ownership rights. Finally, the burden of housing under the old system was left with the state or state-owned enterprises, this was a problem because an obligation to provide housing existed, yet there was an inability to recoup a reasonable return from it. In order for managers and workers to be encouraged to purchase their own houses, a coherent property and land market has to exist.

Urban land use reform began in 1979 when the PRC law on co-operative joint ventures allowed indigenous enterprises to use their land as capital to co-operate with foreign investors. Between 1982 and 1987, pilot schemes in various cities were set up to collect land-use fees. The level of fee related to the land use, amount of supply and infrastructure and the level of fees is shown in Table 3.1.

Table 3.1   Pilot Land Use Fee Schemes

Date of Introduction	Area	Fee Rate yuan/m²/pa	Anount Collected in first year
1982	Shenzhen Special Economic Zone (SEZ)	1 - 4	10m yuan (1982)
1984	Hushuen City (in Liaoning Province, N E China)	0.2 - 0.6	13m yuan (1984)
1984	Guangzhou (only the Economic and Technological Development Districts, new construction projects, foreign investments)	0.5 - 4.0	20m yuan (1984)

From 1987, Shenzhen, one of the first SEZs, began to grant land use rights and the three initial negotiations concerned rights granted to domestic enterprises. These rights are summarised in Table 3.2.

In July 1988, Shanghai granted rights over a piece of land in the Hong Qiao Economic and Technological Development District to a Japanese company through international open tender, the premium for this was paid in US dollars.

Between 1988 and 1990, three major pieces of legislation were passed which consolidated the moves to reform the land market.

In April 1988, the 7th National Peoples' Congress passed a significant amendment to the PRC Constitution which revised article 10, clause 4 of the Constitution to include the right of transfer of land use.

On the 27 September 1988, the State Council promulgated the Tentative Regulations of Land-Use Taxation in Cities and Towns of the People's Republic of China. These taxes are levied on all indigenous profit making enterprises and organisation. The bands of land use tax are:
• Large Cities (>1 million population):   0.5 -10 yuan/m² pa
• Medium Sized Cities (0.5-1m):   0.4 - 8 yuan/m² pa
• Small Cities (0.2-0.5m):   0.3 - 6 yuan/m² pa
• Towns(< 0.2m), industrial and/or mineral regions: 0.2 - 4 yuan/m² pa

Table 3.2   Initial Land Use Rights Granted in Shenzhen

Date	Grantee	
8 September 1987	Shenzhen Industrial Import and Export Corporation of China, National Aeri-Technology Import and Export Corporation	By negotiation: 1322 m^2 residential use 200 yuan/m^2 50 years' rights
15 September 1987	Shenzhen Engineering Development Co.	By tender: 46355 m^2 residential use 368 yuan/m^2 50 years' rights
1 December 1987	Shenzhen SEZ Real Estate Co.	By auction: 8588 m^2 residential use 610 yuan/m^2 50 years' rights

Land is classified into different grades in the various cities and towns and the taxes levied within the bands indicated above according to the grade. To date, the highest tax band of 8 yuan/m^2 pa has been levied in Shanghai. This tax is for indigenous enterprises only, for foreign enterprise a system of land-use fees is levied which is separate and different. For indigenous enterprises the land use taxes replace the land use fees mentioned earlier. However in some cities, like Shenzhen, land use fees are still collected for indigenous land users because the level of the fees is higher than the tax. The fees are shared with the central government on the same basis as the land use tax.

The third piece of legislation passed was in December 1988 when the 5th session of the Standing Committee of the National People's Congress amended the Land Administration Law of the PRC. The significant changes are indicated below:

- the land use rights of state or collective-owned land may be transferred through legal procedures. The detailed methods for land-use right transfers will be regulated by the State Council;
- the state will practice a pay-for-use land system for state-owned land, whereby users will pay for the right to use the land under the regulation of the State Council;

- there will be prohibition of any occupation of state land or land belonging to a commune or sale or letting except in accordance with the law;
- there will be prohibition of use other than the permitted use;
- there will be forfeiture of monetary gain from illegal letting or illegal transfer of land together with fines;
- the use of land by joint venture or foreign companies will be regulated by rules to be made at a later date by the State Council.

The purposes of these changes in the law was to prevent a collapse into anarchy in the land markets by ensuring that changes of use and occupation would have to be approved and registered and that the state would retain the right to recover land required for public works or the needs of state-owned enterprises.

On the 19 May 1990, the State Council promulgated two significant decrees which affected land use and the land market. Decree 55 was the *Provisional regulations on the granting and transferring of land use rights over state owned land in cities and towns.* Decree 56 was the *Provisional measures for the administration of foreign investors to develop and operate plots of land.*

Decree 56 is based on Decree 55 but is used in circumstances to grant large plots of land to foreign developers and encourage them to invest in infrastructure. These areas of land would be more than 1 km² and the developers could assign rights of parts of the land when the infrastructure was completed. The main conditions of Decree 55 are set out in Table 3.3. Decree 55 has popularised the land lease system in China.

Proposals for the Future

Since 1987 there has been a dual track approach to the granting of land use rights and this is whose graphically in Figure 3.1.

The problem of this allocation is that there is an inequality between these approaches. The allocated land users just pay land use tax, the highest of which cannot exceed 200yuan/m² (10yuan/m² pa in perpetuity at 5% = 200yuan/m²) but the highest premium is more than 10,000yuan/m². So the Chinese government is trying to use track (2) shown in Figure 3.1 rather than (1) and now more and more cities have eliminated the allocation of land to non-profit making uses.

Another problem is related to differences in sale prices between

Table 3.3 Decree 55 Provisional Regulations on the Granting and Transferring of Land Use Rights over State-owned Land in Cities and Towns, the State Council of PRC

Article No.	Details
4	Land use rights obtained in accordance with regulations under this decree maybe transferred, assigned, leased or mortgaged or used to develop other economic activities. The legitimate rights and interests of the land owners shall be protected by the laws of the state.
12	The maximum duration for the granting of land use rights are determined by the use of the land as set out below: (i) 70 years for residential use; (ii) 50 years for industrial use; (iii) 50 years for educational, scientific and technological, cultural, health and sports uses; (iv) 40 years for commercial, tourism and recreational activities; (v) 50 years for general or other uses.
13	The land use rights may be granted in any of the following ways: (i) agreement (negotiation); (ii) invitation for bids (tender); (iii) auction.
14	Land users shall, within sixty days after entering into the contract for granting the land use rights, pay the full amount of the land granting fees (premium). In the event that such fees are not paid in full within the time limit, the grantor (the Land Administration Department of the People's Government of Cities and Counties) shall have the right to rescind the contract and may demand compensation for breach of contract.
16	After paying the land granting fees in full, land users shall, in accordance with the regulations, complete the registration and obtain the land use certificate (deeds) for the purpose of acquiring the land use rights.
19	The land use rights of the land which has not been developed and utilised by investment in accordance with the duration and conditions stipulated in the contract for granting land use rights shall not be transferred (including sale, exchange and donation). (Now the government has stipulated that the granted land cannot be transferred until more than 25% of the building cost has been expended.)
39	The land use rights shall terminate for such reasons as the expiration of the duration set forth in the contract for granting land use rights, the revocation of the land use rights or the extinguishment of the land.

negotiation, tender and auction. The differences between these approaches usually mean that negotiation comes to an end with some compromise and the price of land is not negotiated at market prices. At present, more than 99%

of the granted land has been negotiated, but there has now been a call for more land to be granted on a tender or auction basis. Because of the predominance of negotiated prices, the average prices of land granted use rights are low compared to the subsequent prices on transfer. Thus on 13

Figure 3.1 Dual Track System of Granting Land Use Rights (1987-1994)

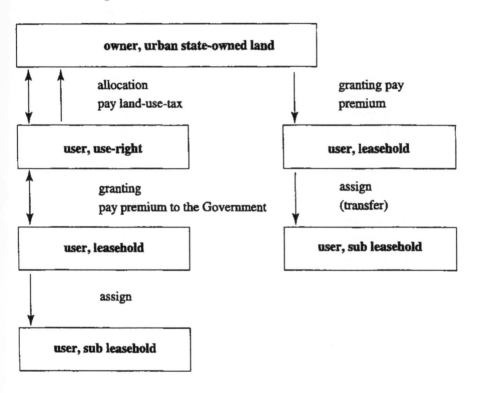

Table 3.4 Rates of Value-added Tax

Profit on resale of Land	Tax Rate
Up to 50%	30%
50% - 100%	40%
100% - 200%	50%
200% +	60%

December 1993, the State Council promulgated the Land value-added tax tentative regulations and these tax rates are set out in Table 3.4 below. The rate is progressive for each range of profit level.

In summary, the effect of urban land reform has had important impact on the economy of the PRC. Urban land reform has provided a supply of land onto the market to establish a functioning property market. It has restrained land use in agriculture diverting land to a higher, more profitable use. However, the amount of arable land used for construction has fallen over the period since 1986 (see Table 3.5).

Over the period from 1988 to 1991 land use tax collected amounted to 8859 million yuan. Land reform has also provided an impetus for redevelopment. If the land was previously allocated by the state, developers just need to pay enough money for demolition and rehabilitation and a nominal premium to get the land, so the prospective users can make a huge profit. Thus in many cities redevelopment projects are more attractive than others.

The process of land development in China is very complicated. The process of land development depends on the way the developer obtains the land, either through allocation/negotiation or by tender/auction. These processes are summarised below in Figure 3.2. Allocation is applicable only where the developer is also an owner occupier. The other methods of negotiation, tender and auction are applicable to any owner occupiers or developers.

Table 3.5   Arable Land Lost per Annum

Year	
1986	9.59 m mu
1987	5.10 m mu
1988	2.91 m mu
1989	1.08 m mu
1990	1.00 m mu

15 mu = 1ha

Figure 3.2 The Process of Land Development in the PRC

Allocation and Negotiation

(i)   Apply for investment planning permission
(ii)   Find a site to meet users' needs
(iii)   Apply for planning permission
(iv)   Purchase the site
(v)   Manage construction phase
(vi)   Use the property for owner occupation

Tender and Auction

(i)   The government will prepare documents for the granting of rights over the land
(ii)   The government put up the documents for public approval
(iii)   Prepare bids
(iv)   Win the competition
(v)   Arrange Finance
(vi)   Purchase the land
(vii)   Develop the land
(viii) Manage the completed property

Source :   [SEPC, 1994].

4 China's Land Reform and the Establishment of a Property Market: Problems and Prospects

As a part of the Chinese economic reform, land reform is necessary to change the previous allocation system to a market driven system. As a result, successive reforms of China's land tenure system have been implemented, culminating in the establishment of a system of 'land use rights' (LURs) which represents the equivalent of a leasehold system. LURs are tradable and in certain cases can be acquired by both domestic and overseas investors.

This chapter examines the political and economic evolution of LURs and from this basis reviews the current state of the market in property in the People Republic of China for both indigenous and overseas investors. The review examines the major problems, which China faces in developing a mature market and the prospects for the emergence of such a market.

The problems of the bureaucratic structure and conflicts within it are highlighted, as are the issues, which have arisen within the housing market. A focus also is provided on the most active region - the Pearl River Delta - and the influence of Hong Kong on both the reforms and the market.

China - A Major Economic Force

A Transformation Unprecedented

China's economic development has been nothing short of phenomenal. Depending on which measure is used, China's economy is ranked either third or tenth largest in the world with output measured at US$1.7 trillion for 1992. At current growth rates the combined economies of China, Hong Kong and Taiwan are predicted to be larger than that of the United States in the early part of the 21st century.

All that from a country that only in 1979 embarked on its open-door policy which included reforms in trade, banking, management and rural development; that established special economic zones only in 1980; whose commune system was abolished only in 1985; where foreign investment was formally encouraged only in 1987; where laws were passed to allow foreign ownership and development of large tracts of land in 1991; where stock markets were established only in 1992; where price controls were largely removed and where the government formally announced its objective of a socially led market economy all within 1994.

Whilst this period has not been without its critical moments, to shift 1.1 billion people spread over 9.6 million square kilometres from a centralised communist economy in stagnation to a more efficient market-oriented economy is unprecedented.

It is perhaps therefore not surprising that structural imbalances have emerged in its economic development. In particular light industry has consistently outpaced the growth of basic industries and there have been serious energy shortages and infrastructure bottlenecks, which have contributed to high inflationary pressures in times of high economic acceleration. This high inflation combined with periods of social unrest has forced the government to follow a 'stop-go' policy throughout the 80's (reminiscent of British economic policy of the 50's and 60's) in which periods of high growth and decentralisation have invariably been followed by a period of suppressed growth and partial recentralisation to allow the economy to cool off.

DENG's Return

The present high growth stage in China's economic development commenced when the then senior leader DENG Xiaoping re-entered the political fray quite unexpectedly in February 1992. This was an attempt to put China back on the reform trail once again following the clampdown on the economy in 1988 and the subsequent clampdown on social unrest in 1989 which saw the revocation of many reform measures.

DENG called for bolder reforms; a policy, which has been met with widespread support both in the established coastal areas but also in the relatively underdeveloped inland provinces and cities. The call for a bolder stance on reforms also served as a signal for foreign investors to return to China encouraged by high growth rates in the south and bank savings of US$182 billion.

Though economic activity has responded enthusiastically to the green-light signal, many of the problems such as structural imbalances leading to high inflation still exist and it is likely that a continuation of the stop-go policy will persist in the near future though hopefully without the extreme policy measures that accompanied it last time. Grey legal areas, an inefficient business environment, a domestic market that is still largely closed and a currency that is not freely convertible are some of the obstacles still to be overcome.

The Socialist Market Economy

But the effects of the renewal of the reform policy can clearly be seen. China has extensively opened its economy, granting autonomy to state-owned enterprises, reduced the administrative powers and personnel of the government and removed price controls. At the 14th Congress of the Chinese Communist Party the concept of 'socialist market economy' was formally acknowledged as the nation's course. Chinese economists have estimated that the market economy has already spread to two thirds of the coastal areas and that China's transformation to a full market economy will be accelerated in the coming years.

High Growth

The main economic indicators are summarised in Table 1.1 in Chapter 1, but the two to focus on are the real GNP growth of 12% for 1994 and the growth in urban consumer price inflation which has risen from 1.3% in 1990 to a forecast rate of 12% for 1996.

Land Reforms

As stated earlier, along side the open-door policy, internal reforms have also taken place. While the overriding characteristic of the economic system of the PRC can be expected to remain communist and consequently centrally state planned, there has been a general move to investigate capitalist economic and management theory and techniques, and to introduce to the domestic market incentive-based systems (which translates directly from the Chinese as 'producing responsibility systems'). The process has been referred to as 'producing capitalism with Chinese characteristics'. These developments have required a reconsideration of land within the economic framework of a Marxist state, and resulted in the acceptance of the concept that the use of land has a value to the user and that PRC commercial and industrial enterprises can purchase and trade in the right to use land.

Private real property rights do not exist in the PRC in the same way as in the capitalist countries of the West. All land is owned by the state and originally the land reforms use the term land-use rights and not the capitalist terms freehold and leasehold. However, the major legislation on land-use rights in 1990 now uses the term lease when referring to the secondary market, but not when the rights are granted by the state - these are still referred to as land-use rights. The establishment of a market in land and property requires a pragmatic view to be taken of Marxism. The PRC has done so treating as a commodity subject to the economic laws of commodities for which there is more ideological flexibility and which, they have decided, allows them to sell land-use rights. It all sounds rather contrived, but at least it has allowed the PRC to get off the ideological hook!

Prior to the open-door policy and consequent economic reforms, the use value of land was established by the state through central economic planning, as there was no market, the price was purely notional. The use to which land was put and the price charged by the state for use of the land (by state institutions as that is all that existed) was decided by a process of 'negotiation and compromise' between the various ranks of cadres and government officials. The objective was simply to resolve their differences, conflicts and interests and, as a market economy did not exist, the price did not represent value as understood in the West.

After the introduction of the open-door policy, the value of the right to use land was recognised, particularly in relation to joint venture enterprises. In addition, state enterprises were required to take responsibility for their own losses and profits. The criteria of competitive performance in deciding rank, bonuses and welfare contributed to keen competition among state enterprises and it has become much more difficult to resolve state enterprises' conflicts and interests merely through 'negotiation and compromise'. As a result, new methods of allocation of land-use rights have been introduced. The PRC has drawn from the experience of Hong Kong in this development as, interestingly, Hong Kong's land is also all owned by the 'state', i.e., the Crown (except for the land on which the Anglican cathedral stands) - a situation which contrasts with its capitalist image.

At present, the charge of a premium for the use of land through negotiation, tender or auction applies only to a small proportion of land in China. Alongside this system, for the majority of land, is a land-use fee system in which indigenous enterprises are charged for the use of the land they occupy on an annual basis. The system is not yet sophisticated and lacks consistency, but is moving towards a system of economic allocation of land.

There are different rates for different uses and locations, and the fee is waived in many circumstances. For example, commercial enterprise may pay full land-use fees, administrative units may pay 50%, land for public housing 20%, schools, parks and temples may be exempt. There may be up to 200% difference between downtown and suburban areas. The fee is usually very low, only a few yuan per square meter per year. A confusion is that often such land-use fees are referred to as annual land and/or property taxes. The latest legislation says that under land-use tax regulations such users have to pay a land-use fee. The terms used, amount levied, exemptions and level of sophistication of the system vary between locations.

When land has been acquired at a premium, an annual land-use fee may or may not be required. It is, it is often only a nominal sum, equivalent to a ground rent in an UK type system.

The Official View

In April 1988, the 7th National People's Congress passed a most significant amendment to the PRC Constitution, which revised Clause 4 of Article 10 from:

> 'No organisation or individual may appropriate, buy, sell or lease or unlawfully transfer land in other ways.'

to:

> 'No organisation or individual may appropriate, buy, sell or lease or unlawfully transfer land in other ways. The right of land use can be transferred in accordance with the law.'

In December 1988, following on from the amendment of Article 10, the 5th Session of the Standing Committee of the 7th National People's Congress subsequently amended the 'Land Administration Law of the People's Republic of China' in a way which further clarified the legality of transferring land-use rights.

It was the first step in reflecting the amendment in the legislation and was at a broadly based philosophical level. It laid down the policies within which subsequent more detailed legislation was to be drafted. The significant provisions were:

- the land-use right of state or collective-owned land may be

transferred through legal procedures. Detailed methods for land-use right transfers will be regulated by the State Council;
- the state practises a paid use land system for state-owned land. Detailed methods of the paid land-use system for state-owned land will be regulated by the State Council;
- prohibition of any occupation of state land or land belonging to a commune, or any sale or letting thereof, except in accordance with the provisions of the law. This clause also empowers the resumption of land belonging to a commune;
- prohibition of the use land other than in line with the permitted use;
- forfeiture of any monetary gain from any illegal letting or any illegal transfer of land together with fines meted out on the people responsible for such transaction;
- provision that the use of land by joint venture companies or foreign companies will be regulated by other rules to be made by the State Council.

The objectives to be achieved by the provisions were that:
- the state or near anarchy in land use and occupation was to be frozen in its present state before it got even worse;
- any change of use or occupation would have to be approved and registered;
- the power of resumption to the state of any land, not just for implementation of any public works scheme, but also for the need of state-owned enterprises, is reserved.

These amendments have been seen as a landmark heralding the formal establishment of a system of private property rights - a real estate market in China (but it may be a real estate market that is significantly different from any other).

According to Marxist theory, land is singled out as incapable of being regarded as a commodity, since it is not a product of man's labour - land exists by itself. Thus, with no one having any title to land and land itself not being accepted as a commodity, it was not surprise that whatever land (or property) market existed prior in China to 1949 quickly disappeared thereafter. The market mechanism was substituted by state allocation of land to the needy, whether it was premises for factories or homes for people. Since no title was given, possession it was nine points of the law; since there was no market, registration even of the possessory title appeared to be of no practical purpose and was, therefore, not carried out (Kan,1989).

The system was soon shown to be inappropriate to the economic reforms taking place in China because:

- the state derived no direct economic benefit from its land holdings although the occupiers of land were able to turn their possession to economic benefit;
- the last of a market deprived both central and local governments of the chance of raising finance through land sales for infrastructure development for enhancement of cities and towns;
- it leads to inefficient use of land resources with under and over use of land and lack of flexibility leading to difficulties in relocation;
- the burden of providing housing lay with the state or state-owned enterprises. This leads to immobility of labour which was frequently tied to state enterprises and a lack of responsibility on the part of the occupiers;
- the system is not conducive to attracting foreign investment into property if land and buildings are held only with an unspecified period of possession and with the occupiers' rights not fully and clearly defined.

The Director of the PRC State Land Administration (SLA) and Chairman of the China Land Society identified that China's reformed land tenure system would have its own characteristics that will produce a market rather different from others. He stated that:

- the reform is not to establish a variety of land ownership forms, e.g., freehold, leasehold. The reform is to commercialise land-use rights, and to apply land rent principles and value laws to the flow of land-use rights;
- the reform is not to weaken state ownership rights of land while strengthening utilisation rights of land; instead, it is to strengthen both. The reform is not to change state ownership of land. To enforce state ownership rights is, on the one hand, to fully actualise such right in an economic sense, and, on the other hand, to have efficient macro-and micro-control of land use;
- the market mechanism is not to be brought to fullest play, but is to be qualified. Not only is there to be no market for free selling and buying g of land, the flow of land-use rights is also not to be completely commercialised. Free allocation of rights shall be continued in certain cases.

The pattern of the reform is to allow the co-existence of two forms of paid land use. One form is collecting annual land taxes, i.e., land-use fees, which, it is said, shall be spread as soon as possible to every city and town and to all factories and mines. The other is to charge a premium (in the words of Wang - 'the form of collecting the total land rent for the entire term of the lease'), which shall be adopted in a few suitable cities.

Such changes have required ideological rationalisation and the Director of SLA does so by saying that: history only finds utopian socialists who claim that the socialist system warrants citizens using public land free of charge. Founders of Marxism foresaw the existence of land rent in a socialist society; even though they thought that society would be incompatible with a commodity economy.

It is felt that China has long misused her urban land, not due to state ownership of land, but due to the free use of land without a fixed duration of use, and that Hong Kong's experience is worthy for China to draw upon.

In Hong Kong, all land is owned by government, outlawing free selling and buying of land or private ownership of land; but because it follows the practice of paid lease and transfer of land-use rights, its land market is well developed and has been a mainstay for the region's rapid social and economic progress. For China, with its long established state ownership of urban land, it is felt that the best mode of reform would be a similar one that both promotes forces of production and maintains state ownership of land.

It is felt that the old land-use system actually deprives the state of its proprietary rights of land, but grants land users such rights. Therefore, the reform should not further diminish the state's legal rights but strengthen them by changing the highly monopolised old system. From a macro-point of view, land owner and land user shall form a lessor-lessee relationship; the owner shall claim land rents from the users, thus actualising its ownership economically. From a micro-point of view, the land owner (the state) can bind land users by setting down such terms as land-use type, duration of house building, conditions for transfer of land-use rights etc..

The right to use land shall also be strengthened as paid transfer of land-user rights shall be allowed. A lessee's land-use right, since he has paid for such long-term right, is a property right rather than a creditor's right. Before the lease expires, he can legally occupy leased land, gain income from such land, and can also sub-lease or mortgage his right to land use. The reform therefore draws a distinction between commercialising urban land, which is unacceptable, and commercialising the rights to use land, which is acceptable. The policy points out that Hong Kong adopts such a system.

The problem of the change-over of land tenure system is recognised by classifying land into 'old land' and 'new land'. 'Old land' is land that has been allocated to the user under the old system for which an annual land-use charge will be levied by the state and a fixed term given. It is expected that this method will eventually disappear as 'old land' acquires a price and is traded. It will be many years before this system can be implemented and it is expected that it will be the next century before use rights for such land are widely traded. 'New land' is land that the state provides. Land users shall pay a premium for the use of such land in the 'pilot cities', e.g., SEZs etc. Annual charges will be made for such land in other areas, presumably in order to control the rate of development. Free allocation of land will continue for government agencies, military and social welfare purposes. A large part of urban land is for residential use. Paid use of land would add to residents' financial burden, which is already heavy enough because of the high rate of inflation. In addition, both the central government and local governments would suffer a financial strain under paid use of land.

It can be seen that China is finding it difficult to set fair standards for land-use charges and for land prices. China would rather have the annual land rent low rather than high. It is considered that too high a land rent would disturb the whole of society and block the way to reform. Yet, a low land rent can be adjusted to a fair one with little inconvenience.

In early 1990, a significant price of legislation was passed entitled Provisional Regulations on the Granting and Transferring of the Land Use Rights over the State-owned Land in Cities and Towns. This legislation, brought together the various regulations used in the cities, economics zones, etc., for the sale of land-use rights, and rationalised and consolidated them for countrywide application.

The regulations include:
- the separation of ownership and the right to use land;
- the right to sell, lease and mortgage land-use rights (LUR);
- registration of LUR;
- details of the contract for the sale of LUR;
- maximum lengths of terms of LUR;
- change of use;
- transfer of LUR (which includes buildings and other structures on the land);
- leasing of LUR, buildings and other structures (but not before development of the land);
- mortgaging of LUR;
- termination of LUR;
- allocation of LUR free of premium (usually for social purposes,

e.g. schools, hospitals), but subject to a nominal land-use fee;
* proceeds of sale LUR to be used to develop towns and cities.

In May 1990, rules were published allowing foreign investors to acquire land-use rights, either independently or in joint ventures, for undeveloped land, which allowed the foreign investors to provide the infrastructure to enhance the value of the land and bring it into economic production. This significant legislation is entitled *Provisional Measures for the Administration of Foreign Investors to Develop and Operate Plots of Land.*

It now appears that the Hong Kong model of land tenure is regarded as suitable for adoption by China because it has the following merits:

* The Hong Kong model, being a leasehold tenure system, allows for absolute perpetual title of land to be vested in the Government as owner of all land. What the people hold is just a leasehold interest. Such a system lends itself to being easily understood in China.
* The Hong Kong model is one that has been well understood and accepted by international investors.
* Because of the resemblance of the two systems, much less effort will be required to move to Hong Kong's system.

Negotiation, Tender and Auction

The initial experiments involved disposal by negotiation. In fact this did not differ markedly from the conventional 'negotiation and compromise' method previously used, but nevertheless it was enshrined within the land management reform legislation.

This method is utilised for transactions including:

* government or military institutions;
* public administrations or public utilities;
* government subsidised institutions for the development of science, education, public health, or sport facilities.

The basic principle is simply to recoup the funds incurred in preparation of the particular piece of land, via a single premium to be paid by the user for the land-use right.

The second experiment involves the sale of land-use rights by tender and is the preferred method. The tender documents contain several constraints on the development of the land and require bidders to submit, within their tender, an outline design, which complies with the conditions.

The third and most recent of the experiment was to dispose of land by auction but this method has been discontinued. The historic first auction was for a site of 8,588 m² with land-use rights for 50 years for residential purposes and took place on 1 December 1987 in the Shenzhen City Hall.

The Bureaucratic System

There are many stories surrounding the complex and low efficiency of the bureaucratic structure. Many of these stories are true and in considering that there are 28 million Chinese bureaucrats it is perhaps hardly surprising. The message here is that an investor must spend time to understand the organisational structure and the administrative relationship in the Chinese bureaucracy and also spend some time locating key personnel.

The highest administrative authority concerning land is the State Land Administration (SLA), which was established in 1986 under Article 5 of the *Land Administration Law of the People's Republic of China*. Its role is to:

- organise central land-use planning;
- prepare policies, laws and regulations and enforce them;
- arrange land registration, statistics and investigations;
- co-ordinate matters relating to land administration and settle disputes and deal with illegal occupation of land.

Operating at the state level the administration is concerned with the broad management of land mainly in the area of policy. Implementation of policy is carried out in the provinces, districts, cities and autonomous regions. A confusion is that the provinces, cities, etc., often adopt different names for their local land administration bureaux.

Legislation on land matters follows a similar pattern to the organisations, which administer the law. *The Land Administration Law of the People's Republic of China*, which is the highest authority, was made by the State Council and resembles statements of general policy and guidelines. This law requires detailed implementing regulations to be made by the lower levels of regional governments. The lower the level of government, the more detailed the provisions usually are, as they interpret the way in which national provisions will be applied in the local context. In case of conflict between the two sets of law, those published by the superior law-making organ will prevail.

The SLA recognises the great significance of a proper legal framework for land-use rights. Whilst the state law is on the statute book much still remains to be done to reflect its spirit at the local level. There is a great variation at this level from the well developed and detailed regulations of Shanghai and Shenzhen to many areas where local regulations do not exist in any form.

However, relationships between the existing authorities tend to overlap and confusion exists, especially in relation to the SLA and the Ministry of Construction (which includes the Real Estate Administration and Urban Planning Administration). For instance, the State Land Administration, through its local bureaux, is responsible for the transfer of land-use rights - representing the government according to *Land Administration Law*. In some cities, however, the local construction commission also seeks to perform this role because they hold all the registration information relating to buildings and landed property. It is considered urgent, therefore, for the government to clarify the jurisdiction and function of each authority, and to designate a unified, powerful authority to take over the responsibility for land and property administration and construction.

All local and foreign entities can acquire land-use-rights, with the exception of companies, which are incorporated in countries, which have no diplomatic or official trade relations with the PRC. They may be barred from entering the market. Local land administration bureaux at or above county level have the authority to grant land. Their role is to:

- grant land-use-rights;
- organise central land-use-planning;
- prepare and enforce policies, law and regulations about the use of land;
- arrange land registration, statistics and investigations;
- co-ordinate matters relating to land administration and settle disputes and deal with illegal occupation of land.

The user of land shall, after paying in the full cost of the grant of the leasehold, carry out registration procedures in accordance with regulations, obtain a land use certificate and thereby acquire the right to use certificate and thereby acquire the right to use the land. After acquiring the land-use-rights, the user signs a contract with the land administration bureau specifying the rights and obligations of both parties. The development must be completed in accordance with the time limit stipulated in the contract otherwise the bureau has the right to terminate the contract and exercise the right of re-entry. If developers wish to change the use of the land specified in the contract they are required to seek the approval from the bureau and pay a premium which is equivalent to the difference in the prevailing land prices and to sign a supplementary contract.

Housing

Of those buildings completed for the market in 1992 the residential sector accounted for approximately 82% which was marginally down from 1991. But in the so-called 'hot-spots' (the coastal areas and major inland cities) the proportions of buildings completed for the different sectors are very different. In Hainan for example residential properties accounted for only 65% of the marketable buildings completed with a similar proportion in Shenzhen, 78% in Guangzhou and 50% in Xiamen.

These figures illustrate that the demand pattern is changing as local economies develop and grow. In particular as an increase its exposure to overseas investment so the need for purpose built office buildings as well as shops for commercial and service industries rises dramatically.

However if they are to avoid social unrest housing will remain a priority for Government as the economy grows. The legacy of China's mixed ideology is reflected in the actual market practice in that, in order to keep the market supply in balance, the government is separating the residential market into different 'sectors', each differentiated by price control or regulation. Therefore, for the lowest income group, there is 'welfare housing', and for the relatively better-off group or those working in favoured industries, e.g. in the high-tech industries, there is 'minimal profit housing' which allows developers only a minimal profit margin. For the 'actual market' or the commodity housing sector, there are a further two sub-sectors; namely 'internal market commodity housing' and 'external market commodity housing'. Foreigners (including foreign Chinese) can only purchase the latter sub-sector. These two sub-sectors are the actual market because they are more frequently traded and prices are more or less adjusted by the market demand and supply, with the exception of the artificial price ceiling control in the internal market. Hence, the inter-market price differentiation is quite sub substantial, e.g., in Shenzhen City in Guangdong Province, residential price for the internal commodity market is about 1/5 to 1/9 of that of the external commodity market. In terms of residential development several distortions emerged over 1991/92 as investment flowed into the higher priced end of the residential market targeting overseas investors. What has been recognised perhaps a little too late in some areas is that the buyer market at this price level is limited. Markets particularly in the South have become overheated. Prices have soared to levels that are way beyond the means of domestic purchasers and the fact that 80,000 villas were recently made available for the market in Hong Kong and that 30,000 only were sold is testimony to the somewhat speculative nature of this sector. When you also consider that more than 200,000 villas are projected to be built in Zhejiang, Shanghai and Jiangsu the seriousness of this distortion becomes self-evident.

The Front-line Markets

China's developing market structure can be witnessed virtually everywhere as province competes with province for much needed foreign investment and provinces invest in other provinces increasing the domestic flow of capital.

The whole of the east coast from Dalian to Bohai, some 2,800 km of coastline is now open for investment pulling in large sums of money. Shanghai is spearheading a major inroad westwards to the central provinces along the Changjiang better known in the West as the Yangtse River. This will connect with the strategic city of Wuhan and accelerate the development of Hubei province and eventually Chongqing in Sichuan province. Shanghai together with pearl River Delta and Beijing represented the three front-line markets as major gateways to China. They have the greatest potential for reforming the real estate markets in China.

The Pearl River Delta area embracing the area market by Guangzhou, Shenzhen and Zhuhai. This is the gateway to the south of China and indeed through its coalescence with Hong Kong has already facilitated market reforms throughout the rest of China.

The municipality of Shanghai is the gateway to the heart of China. The development of the Pudong area and eventual redevelopment of Puxi plus the opening up of the Yangtse will see Shanghai re-emerge as one of the major financial and industrial centres of Asia. Its location and links westwards along the Yangtse into the heart of China to other strategic cities such as Wuhan with its North-South connections and eventually Chongqing will facilitate development of the inland provinces.

Beijing and its sister city of Tianjin (both municipalities) not only represent the political centre and major industrial region of China but are seen also as the gateway to the North facilitating the development of real estate markets in Hebei, Shanxi and Liaoning.

The three together will play vital roles as China develops and reforms its market structure throughout this decade and takes major steps towards the development of its socialist market economy. But the focus in this paper i the Pearl River Delta as the pre-eminent economic growth area of China.

The Pearl River Delta

The Pearl River Delta is a loosely defined geographical area in the southern part of China. Three major rivers converge in the area and form the delta, the Xi Jiang (River West); Bei Jiang (River North) and Dong Jiang (River East) Three strategic points define the boundary. Guangzhou in the North and Shenzhen and Zhuhai on the east and west of the delta respectively. Within this triangle lies Guangzhou City; two special economic zones (SEZs) Shenzhen SEZ and Zhuhai SEZ and 28 other open economic cities and counties with a total area of 47,400 km². It contains about 20.8 million people or 33% of the total provincial population and accounts for about 26% of the provincial area. Administratively, the delta area lies in jurisdiction of Guangdong Province, which is the highest level of regional government structure.

The Delta's principal strategic value lies in the special relationship that it has both culturally and economically with Hong Kong. It is this that kept the Pearl River Delta and the rest of Guangdong Province ahead of the pack.

Growth

Table 4.1 on illustrates how rapid growth has been in the major cities with GDP growth averaging between 12% and 42% p.a. over the 80's with the two SEZs of Shenzhen and Zhuhai in the lead.

Infrastructure

Figure 4.1 summarises the major infrastructure works. The majority will be taking place in and around Guangzhou city with Shenzhen and Zhuhai consolidating on their position of already having developed their infrastructure over the last 10 years. Guangzhou has been neglected in this respect and is making a serious attempt to catch up.

Activity in the Delta

This section can give no more than the briefest snapshot in which Table 4.2 indicates the asking prices of different properties in the Delta region.

Although they only represent the asking prices, they illustrate the current state of the structure of the market in the sense that a secondary market, especially in the retail and office sectors, has not yet fully developed and asking prices are the principal market indicators available.

Table 4.1   Growth of GDP in Eight Major Cities in the Pearl River Delta

	1980 In million Yuan	1985 In million Yuan	1990 In million Yuan	1991 In million Yuan	Per annum average increase 1980 - 90	Per annum average increase 1990 - 91
Guangzhou	5754.97	12436.23	31959.52	38667.41	11.7%	16.3%
Shenzhen	270.12	3324.45	13585.88	17481.63	41.86%	24.8%
Zhuhai	375.28	1030.82	4119.31	6049.07	24.77%	59.4%
Huizhou	720.00	1430.00	4879.13	6142.53	13.09%	23.9%
Dongguan	704.40	2037.84	6461.50	7484.15	–	15.5%
Zhongshan	635.21	1729.90	4354.67	5266.88	16.08%	21.5%
Jiangmen	1782.16	3640.75	9308.94	11037.38	14.60%	18.7%
Foshan	1677.31	4809.97	12549.80	16663.85	17.12%	30.0%
Total	11919.45	30439.96	87217.75	108792.90		

Source : Investment Guide to the Pearl River Delta 1992.

Guangdong: The Delta's Hinterland

In the past ten years, the whole province has developed over 290 small residential neighbourhoods each with an average area of about 30,000 m² (50 have been developed in Shenzhen , and 35 in Guangzhou city). The province has embarked on a comprehensive land use survey (1993) which when complete will form the basis of future land supply policy. Total land supply for real estate development in Guangdong in 1993 will be controlled within a total of 30.6 million m², which represents approx. 50% of 1992's supply. It is estimated that of the land supplied in 1992 about 30 million m² remains undeveloped. Hence, the total supply of land for development in 1993 will be more or less the same as in 1992.

In 1992, Guangdong Province, saw some 62km² of land developed, 3 times more than the year before. There was about 17.4 million m² of property sold, again, 3 times more than 1991. Of this total floor area, 15% was developed by the State, while 85% by private developers both local and foreign. But this high level of activity has not been without its problem hence the recent controls on speculation which mean that land use rights now can only be transferred after 25% of total investment stipulated in the land sale conditions has been expended in addition to the price of the land.

In terms of development potential, Guangdong has topped the league in absorbing Hong Kong investment funds. It is estimated to have absorbed 62% of total Hong Kong investment in China, way ahead of its two major competitors namely Shanghai and Fujian. In terms of infrastructure, Guangdong also receives a major share, about 52% of the total number of projects involving Hong Kong investment, or 72% by project costs.

Of the known investments Hong Kong investors have involvement in over 400 projects in Guangdong at a total project cost of HK$320 billion with property investment accounting for some 210 projects covering 750 million sq.ft. of land and provide 840 million sq.ft. of floor space at a total project cost of some HK$134 billion.

Shenzhen tops the league in all sectors which is to be expected given its links and proximity to Hong Kong, its special status and its newly developed economic base. Next to Shenzhen is Guangzhou where property prices are rapidly catching up, again, given its economic development and historical importance in the Province. The other cities are active at much lower price level reflecting largely the relative lack of infrastructure provision. Table 4.3 shows planned investment in the major Delta markets from Hong Kong.

From the above, of the total potential (known) investment of HK$41.4 billion that is being directed into the Delta's property markets, Guangzhou accounts for the largest share, (44% of the total) while Shenzhen accounts for a relatively modest 25%. This represents the fact that development opportunities in Shenzhen are now being limited by its geographical size and a twelve-year history of rapid development. Whereas in Guangzhou which has largely been neglected by investors over the 80's and given its size, historical and economic importance in the Delta area has become relatively attractive to investors.

Figure 4.1   Infrastructure Developments in the Pearl River Delta

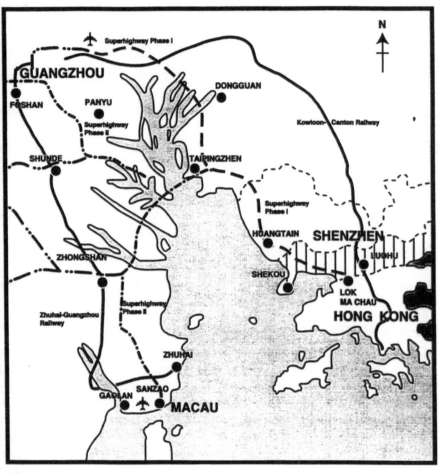

Source :   *'Urban Housing Reforms in China', World Bank staff report, World Bank, Washington D.C.*

Table 4.2   Asking Prices of Different Properties in the Major Delta Cities as at May 1993

City	Residential US$/sq. ft	Commercial US$/sq. ft	Retail US$/sq. ft
Shenzhen	120 - 120	200 - 300	400 - 800
Guangzhou	90 - 120	170 - 320	250 - 500
Zhuhai	50 - 80	90 - 140	140 - 220
Panyu	30 - 60	-	-
Zhongshan	40 - 80	-	130 - 260
Dongguan	30 - 50	-	-
Shantou	60 - 80	50 - 60	80 - 180

Source : Bank of East Asia China Division.

The urban area of Guangzhou is very densely populated and redevelopment of the inner area is a major initiative prompted by government. It also provides a major opportunity for developers. The major redevelopment areas include Yuexiu, Dongshan, Haizhu and Liwan and the city government has been very receptive in co-operating with foreign investors to redevelop these areas. For instance, in the first half of 1992, nine parcels of land (a total area of 627,000 m^2) on Dongfeng Road were sold to foreign developers for mixed redevelopment project of residential/commercial buildings. More recent attention has been placed on the area along the line of the proposed underground railway. To improve living conditions in the city the government is planning to double the urban area while at the same time trying to keep the urban population more or less constant.

The plans for Guangzhou are ambitious and if everything is accomplished it will be good in the long-term. However, the market potential in Guangzhou is not without its problems. The recent tightening of credit has made developers anxious in terms of selling their developments as quickly as

Table 4.3 Planned Investment in the Delta Property Market by Hong Kong Investors

	Total investment planned (US$ million)
Guangzhou	2360
Shenzhen	1370
Dongguan	1060
Huizhou	380
Zhuhai	90
Zhongshan	40
Total	5300

Source : Hong Kong Research, Credit Lyomais Securities, May 1993.

Note : These figures are indicative only of Hong Kong's investor activity. These figures are not exhaustive and the bars are for illustrative purposes only (not to scale).

possible. This is because when bank financing is more difficult to obtain, pre-selling becomes their major source of finance. Some developers have even tried to sell their developments before obtaining the necessary documentation and approvals for pre-sales whilst others have been trying to sell before infrastructure or utilities have been developed.

Residential prices in Shenzhen are always high compared to the other Delta cities. In 1993, 7.1 million m² of land will be put on the market, of which 321,000 m² will be put up for tender of which 93,000 m² will be available for foreign investors, i.e. more or less one third. It is estimated that 6.6 million m² of residential floor space will be developed this year and about half will be available for pre-sale. However, only 1.22 million m² will be made available for the external market.

The internal market however is gaining in importance. In February 1993, for instance, there were about 63 transactions completed in Hong Kong dollars while 136 transactions were completed in Renminbi yuan. In some of the more recent developments (where there are both internal and external commodity units available in the same development), the response from the internal market has been far more active than in the external market. This has much to do with the rapid devaluation of the Yuan, which makes property investment by local residents more appealing. Secondly, the external market is more or less flooded after 85,000 units were pushed on to the Hong Kong market last year.

Shenzhen has always had the special benefit of being closest to Hong Kong. As 1997 approaches, the two places are becoming more and more inter-mingled economically, and hence more and more Hong Kong residents are considering buying flats over the border for their own occupation.

Conclusion

The emergence of real estate markets in China to their current stage of development has been nothing short of astonishing particularly in the absence of any concept of market structure. It has been estimated that the total value of arrangements signed in China in respect of real estate development projects in 1992 was worth US$11 billion. The future looks promising. The markets are getting themselves more organised, the regulatory framework is improving. As China takes its place in the world economic system investment in China is inevitable.

It is critical in trying to assess the scale of change in China to distinguish between behaviour and structure (institutional). The behaviour of individuals, firms, etc., gives the appearance that the semblance of a market has formed. People to all intents and purposes buy and sell apartments. Firms to all intents and purposes buy land, build factories and operate those factories. They utilise foreign currency and can be repaid in foreign currency. To all intents and purposes the behaviour of individuals, firms, certain government officials and even the language used in defining policy, i.e., 'responsibility contracts' would support the view that a market in real estate is emerging a system that foreign investors can work within; where capitalists can utilise labour for their own ends (profits).

But the institutional structure has not yet fundamentally changed. For the time being China remains a centrally planned economy with a system based on socialist principles. The Communist Party is still conservative in nature and will for the foreseeable future remain so. As DENG Xiaoping himself said,

'The existing political system has now proved to be a formidable constraint to furthering the course of economic reform.'

The activities seen as the 'market at work' involve only a minute part of the overall stock of land and property in China's vast urban complex and still further is only one small component of a complete market system. But at its current stage of development investors need to be careful. The real estate market is immature in the western context. Local regulations and local practices quite often in practical terms outweigh national regulations. It is therefore extremely difficult to generalise a set of investment rules for cities in China. Investors should see China as consisting of a vast number of different regions and they need to employ a variety of tactics.

One major problem still is the question of property rights. It remains a major stumbling block in the development of a second hand market. Minor local disturbances have erupted in Guangdong Province as a result of disputes between the relevant authorities and residents over unclear delineation of property rights. Developers must therefore pay particular attention to the establishment of title to the land before committing funds. Without a clear definition and protection of property rights real estate development will continue to be the playground of developer/speculators rather than end-users.

Systematic analysis of demand and supply is also a major problem. Due to the long history of planned allocation of land use the existing city structures are far from ideal conforming more to administrative priorities than market forces. On the demand side one key factor is the continued market reform and wider acceptance of China's political route to a 'socialist market economy'. On the supply side however until the markets consolidate and sufficient is known about their mechanisms this will continue to be a problem. Data is always a stumbling block as far as market research is concerned.

A further major inhibition to a mature market is that Renminbi is not a freely convertible currency, and purchases may be made at the official exchange rate or the 'unofficial' exchange rate between which there is a substantial gap. Similarly the ability to convert income in Renminbi into foreign currency and its transfer overseas may be limited in many cases. Such constraints affect the market in real property, particularly for foreign investors. The achievement of a fully developed international market will only be possible with a more long-term development of the economy as a whole and with the consequential ability to ease restrictions on convertibility of Renminbi and provide access to foreign currencies. Alternatively, if a market restricted only to PRC investors is required, it is likely to take much long to develop and be less dynamic in the short to medium term.

The reform of the economy in the PRC must continue for the real estate market to develop. This will require competition between companies, both state and private, without too many state-imposed restrictions and will need consequential changes in attitudes. The problems ahead are extremely complex and require reform of the price system and wage structure. Inflation continues to be a severe problem also and the success of the embryo real estate market is dependent upon the solution of such macroeconomic problems within the constraints of political and ideological pressures, which are unprecedented.

That so much has been achieved in such a short pace of time within a relatively immature system and with people who supposedly lack experience in real estate markets is testimony to the receptiveness of the system to new concepts. China markets however are not for the faint-hearted. They are high risk-high return. Overseas investors should beware but more importantly they should be aware of the pitfalls.

5 Pricing of Land in China's Reforms

Before transition to a market economy, China, in common with other socialist centrally planned economies, regarded land as non-tradable. Theories of land price behaviour were not seen to be relevant under socialist economies. However, the 'modernisations' in China have generated land use right reforms, which accept the concept of land value and generate the need for land pricing.

This chapter discusses the attempts by the Chinese authorities to develop a guideline land price system at the beginning of the land use rights reforms to reflect the official view of the pricing of land. To explain the Chinese authorities' approach, an examination of the socialist economic concept of value as a whole is conducted to illustrate how official thinking is influenced by economic traditions. Although the guideline land price system is not mandatory in China's market system, it does reflect the official view of the theoretical behaviour of market land prices. The pricing of many commodities in China is still to a certain extent a policy rather than a market phenomenon. A similar approach pervades the guideline land pricing system. An examination of this official view of land price may explain some of the reasons for the specific land price behaviour resulting from the privatisation of land use rights in China.

The Concept of Value under Socialist Economies

The first step requires an understanding of the socialist economic view of value, which still dominates China's interpretation of market value. Basically, the origin of the socialist (or Marxist) economic theories of value stem from Ricardo's theories, which are essentially about labour-embodied value (Stigler,1952). It is therefore necessary to look at the Ricardian view on value, although Ricardian theory does not equate directly with socialist economic theory. To Ricardo, the amount of society's labour time allocated to the production of a commodity is the true source of value and also the best measure of value. The only circumstance which could change the natural value of a commodity is a change in the way it is produced and hence the change of labour time required for its production. Lichtenstein (Lichtenstein,1983) classifies this as the objective theory of value which he regards as:

> The source of value must be sought in the sphere of production rather than the sphere of exchange and it is the actual expenditure of human effort which confers value on commodities.

It is an objective theory because the price level is governed by the technical (objective) conditions of production which include the way production is organised within enterprises, the types of technology used, the productivity of the labour force, and the quality and availability of capital and natural resources. These factors are decided exogenously in the labour market, the raw materials market and the technology market.

However, Ricardo only focuses on commodities the supply of which can only be increased by the application of human effort (Lichtenstein,1983) he assumes those commodities which derive their value from scarcity alone form a very small part of the mass of commodities in the market. As mentioned earlier, as the Marxist economic view is based to a certain extent on the Ricardian view, the Marxist frame of reference also excludes goods such as natural resources, land and capital from contributing to value (Brabant,1987).

This objective view of value is obviously inadequate in terms of its explanatory power as far as land in an urban market economy is concerned. The objective theory encompasses only the production side of the commodity not the exchange side. Value therefore, in the Marxist economic view, represents the amount of labour expended on production only without any reference in the market, as Abraham-frois and Berrebi (Abraham-frois,1979) note:

> For Marx, the measure of value exists before exchange. It becomes plain, that it is not the exchange of commodities which regulates the magnitude of their value; but, on the contrary, that it is the magnitude of their value which controls their exchange proportions.

This objective view of value does not capture the nature of value. What the objective theory of value argues is the way value is built up. It fails to look at the purpose of establishing the value of a commodity. The difference lies in the matter of scarcity, both in the sphere of production and the sphere of exchange. Such scarcity of resources in relation to demand generates a need to provide a quantitative measure of value for the priority allocation of resources. Such a need arises through the necessity to express the value concept in a common way in the market to facilitate the efficient flow of exchange of products and resources.

This is especially true in the land market as production cost and exchange value often vary substantially due to the scarcity factor. In some narrower definition, land does not even possess a production cost function. Therefore, in the core of the objective theory of value, only those commodities that enter into production command value. This explains the fact that in the past no monetary value was recognised in the process of the allocation of land in the Chinese economy.

Any commodity that is to enter into the sphere of exchange will invariably require a value to be assigned in order to have a common basis in exchange. The process of assigning value (or valuation process) will invariably involve quantifying the variables that make up the commodity's value basis. It is the choice of these variables that makes the valuation process different under different ideologies. In the socialist economies, these elements invariably evolve around the sphere of production which is theoretically acceptable for most commodities that go through production function for their existence. For those commodities which do not go through a production function, such as land, no such variables are available. The socialist economic view of value, which concentrates on the objective judgement of value, therefore lacks the vision of the inter-relationship between the sphere of production and the sphere of exchange for these kinds of commodities.

In a socialist economy, therefore, market elements are not fundamental to the formation and determination of value. However, in any economy where a market mechanism exists and is relied on to allocate resources, even if such a mechanism accounts for only a small portion of the total economy, such an objective view of value is bound to be illogical. Abraham-frois and Berrebi (Abraham-frois,1979) comment that:

> The case of land and natural resources, the prices of these commodities, which have never been produced, are exclusively determined by their expected conditions of utilisation, i.e., their rent or quasi-rent, are determined by the series of their net returns at the current rate of interest.

China is striving to move to a more market orientated economy, nevertheless much thinking in relation to land value is underpinned by these traditional socialist concepts of value. It is important to understand the means by which such concepts are embodied in the guideline land price system known as Benchmark Pricing, in order to understand the way in which land value is currently being established in China.

The Land Use Rights Reforms

Before the reform, land allocation was taken as part of national or regional economic planning and investment. Hence, a set of socialist economic variables had to be considered before a decision on the distribution or transfer of land could be made. In actual fact, such decisions were the end result of the planned economic investment process and the allocation of land was dependent on overall national economic interests.

To achieve an allocation of land, the applicant must first seek help from the government planning agencies and the corresponding superior government agency. Considerations were given to the amount of investment from the central government as part of the State economic plan and the priority of construction projects in the plan. Once the application for the allocation of land was approved, the amount of land to be allocated would be decided by some empirical ratio between the construction project and its land use acreage.

In this respect, land development decisions were never made on their own merits but only incidental to the need of construction projects. It should be noted that construction projects in China usually refer to heavy industry or large scale infrastructure projects. Seldom was the term construction used to refer to real estate development. When land is regarded as free in the decision making and investment process, it will certainly create problems in the utilisation of land resources.

This can be analysed from different viewpoints. Tang (Tang,1989) examines one of the major problems and terms it as public squatting, by this he refers to:

> The behaviour of public entities rather than that of private individual. The logic of public squatting is that a publicly owned firm is automatically entitled to a piece of land for its production.

When there is such an automatic allocation of resources especially to the state-owned enterprises, it is very easy to have mis-use of and over-demand for them. Moreover, as the cost of acquisition of these resources is never allocated to the production function, spurious profit for these enterprises is easily created. Compounding this, some of these resources may become the assets of the enterprises without entering into the asset value of the firms.

Tang (Tang,1989) gives an example to illustrate this kind of voluntary waste. In Dalian a research institute once asked for approval for a 50,000 m² building site when it only required 600 m² Moreover, according to Tang's research, in Shenyang between 1955 and 1963, each additional 100 million Renminbi Yuan of industrial output value corresponded to an 11 ha. increase in the area of land for industrial use. However, between 1964 and 1978, the efficiency rate dropped to 19 ha. for each increment of 100 million Yuan of industrial output. Discounting the effect of the actual expansion need, the increase in the ha./industrial output ratio is still very substantial, demonstrating a wasteful use of land.

Accompanying this is the break down of the urban land use mechanism which allocates land to different uses according to the needs of each user. One of the most efficient ways of allocating land to different users is to allow bid rent activities to take place. When the activities are able to locate at the desired site, their economic efficiency as well as income earning capacity can improve. This can be a self-enhancing process and depends on the common media of measurement standard - market rent. Rent depends on the actual demand and supply for different uses. When the actual profit earning capacity of different industries cannot be identified accurately and when there is substantial rent control on all properties, it is very difficult to relate location, land use and land value in a logical way.

Urban land use cannot be efficient without such a measurement standard when land occupation does not involve a monetary cost. The result is that competition for land use depends mainly on the priority given by the State administration to various enterprises. One direct result has been residential land being squeezed by industrial projects. According to Yang and Liu (Yang,1991), industrial land use counts for 20.5% of the total city centre area in Shanghai; 30.3% in Guangzhou and 34.15% in Fushun. Tang (Tang,1989) gives similar findings that in Liaoning Province, 84% of the 5000 factories in ten cities are located in the cities proper and mixed with residential buildings.

This inefficient land supply mechanism affects not only the private investment incentive in real estate, but also the efficiency of public sector's investment in real estate development. There is in fact a dilemma for the State that, on the one hand, it has to provide housing to the public as welfare, but on the other, because land has no monetary value, the State gets no direct revenue from it. Such a situation causes the government to carry a substantial burden in investment in housing.

The overriding characteristic of the economic system in the PRC is that it is a communist, centrally state-planned economy. Therefore, any reform in the property market will have to be based on socialist principles and amendments will therefore evolve around this ideology.

In April 1988, Clause 4 of Article 10 of the Constitution of the PRC was amended such that:

> No organisation or individual may appropriate, buy, sell, or unlawfully transfer land in other ways. The right of land use can be transferred in accordance with the law.

The addition of the last sentence makes it possible for the real estate market to operate in a manner similar to that of Hong Kong (Walker,1994). Ownership of land still belongs to the State (people), and so there is no conflict to the basic socialist doctrine. However, an element called the Land Use Rights (LURs) was separated out from the bundle of rights associated with the use of land and became the main core of the reform. Under *the Provisional Regulations on the Granting and Transferring of the Land Use Rights over the State-owned Land in Cities and Towns promulgated in 1990*, LURs were separated from ownership rights and became tradable in the market by private treaty; negotiation and auction. LURs are rights with time limits for different kinds of land use (e.g. in some cities, 70 years for residential, 50 years for industrial and 30 years for commercial/office). Moreover, LURs are capable of being mortgaged and transferred.

LURs became China equivalent of the Hong Kong leasehold interest. Fees became payable for the use, grant and transfer of LURs. At the beginning of the reform, land use fees were charged only in new development areas, i.e., land with development potential and capable of being transferred from agricultural use. Land that had already been administratively allocated for a particular development before the reform was not charged. However, when the use of such land is transferred, it will be transformed into LURs under the reform, after a suitable land premium has been paid to the State.

It should be noted that the reform did not come out as a single package. It was a gradual process of changes including the management of land use; separation of land use rights from the main core of property rights;

mechanisms for the transfer and trading of such LURs; reforms in housing allocation, rent level and property taxes, and last and most importantly, reform of the pricing of real estate. This process is known as the 'commercialisation of real estate'. For real estate to be commercialised and traded like other commodities requires an essential element of monetary value to act as a standard measurement as well as the media of exchange.

The Property Market

The real estate industry is an important element in most economies. But such importance was never reflected in China's economy prior to the reform. Before 1987 the portion of the real estate industry in the GNP of the PRC was only around 3-4%, which was substantially lower than most of the East European socialist countries. This had everything to do with the sensitivity of private land ownership in China's political history. In the past, the doctrine of socialism was very much against private land ownership for it created a privileged class of people who could exploit the hard labour of tenants. Not only was private ownership denounced from social point of view, it was also regarded as undesirable in an economic sense.

The legacy of China's mixed ideology is reflected in the actual market practice in that, in order to keep the market supply in balance, the government is separating the residential market into different 'sectors', each differentiated by price control or regulation. Therefore, for the lowest income group, there is 'welfare housing', and for the relatively better off group or those working in favoured industries, e.g., in the high-tech industries, there is 'minimal profit housing' which allows developers only a minimal profit margin. For the 'actual market' or the commodity housing sector, there are a further two sub-sectors; namely 'internal market commodity housing' and 'external market commodity housing'. Foreigners (including foreign Chinese) can only purchase the latter sub-sector. These two sub-sectors are the actual market because they are more frequently traded and prices are more or less adjusted by the market demand and supply, with the exception of the artificial price ceiling control in the internal market.

Due to this price differentiation, the housing market is divided into different 'price zones' each influenced by different demand and supply factors, e.g., the external commodity housing market is to a very large extent influenced by speculative and investment funds from Hong Kong, Taiwan and overseas, and hence very much depend on the economy of these places.

On the other hand, the internal commodity housing market is targeted at real users in China.

Tables 5.1 and 5.2 show market activities in the secondary and tertiary markets in the residential sector in Shenzhen Special Economic Zone immediately over the border from Hong Kong. The secondary market in China means direct sales from developers to the first batch of buyers of their properties. This group of buyers can be end users, investors, speculators or enterprises buying quarters for their employees. The tertiary market represents the exchange between second hand buyers. In the secondary market, the consideration involved in transactions in the external market (which conducts business in either HK$ or US$) for outweighs that of the internal market (in RMB Yuan, the Chinese currency) even though the floor area involved is very similar. This is even more obvious when looking at Table 5.2 where actual market activities can be seen. This table shows that both the money involved in the external market transactions and floor area transacted is greater than for the internal market. This represents substantial speculation or 'investment' from outside China in the market.

Since foreigners cannot buy internal commodity housing, and since there is price control in this market, few foreign developers actually channel their investment into this sub-sector of the market   where there is real and substantial demand   (let alone the fact that the government also limits the land supply to foreign developers e.g. in the land supply plan for Shenzhen in 1993, of the total 321,000 m² of land to be put on the market, only about 93,000 m² will be available to foreign investors). Again, this causes a very serious imbalance of investment.   For example, in the first 10 months of 1992, about 70,000 residential units were being marketed in Hong Kong with a future potential supply by some major Hong Kong developers in China of almost 280 million m² of development rights. One cannot help wondering how the various elements of this kind of planned market development can merge.

Not only do we find such discrepancy in property transaction activities, but also in the leasing market. Table 5.3 shows the rental index, with base year in 1984, for commodity office buildings in the two major commercial districts (Luohu and Futian) in Shenzhen. While the rental index for office buildings leased in Yuan in the internal market has been rising rapidly in recent years compared to the external market leased in HK dollar, the capital values of office buildings show the reverse. This could of course attribute to the relatively higher quality of construction materials used in office buildings for the external market. But such a great discrepancy cannot be justified by this reason alone.

Table 5.1 The Secondary Market in the Commodity Residential Housing Sector in Shenzhen in 1991

Market	Number of Transactions	Area (sq. m)	Currency used	Money involved	Highest price / sq. m	Lowest price / sq. m	Average price / sq. m
Internal	826	110304.5	Yuan	175 803 625.27 (US$ 17 580 363)	15 799.18 (US$ 1 580)	598.2 (US$ 59.8)	1 593.8 (US$ 160)
External	1231	109177.8	HK$	430 881 699.42 (US$ 55 38 325)	24783.86 (US$ 3 186)	938.96 (US$ 121)	3 946.61 (US$ 507.3)
External	13	928.8	US$	549.215	646.83	607.02	639.77

Exchange Rate in 1991 : US$1 : 10 Yuan, and US$1 : HK$7.78

Source : Shenzhen Real Estate Market Yearbook 1992

Table 5.2   The Tertiary Market in the Commodity Residential Housing Sector in Shenzhen in 1991

Market	Number of Transactions	Area (sq. m)	Currency used	Money involved	Highest price / sq. m	Lowest price / sq. m	Average price / sq. m
Internal	339	343349.2	Yuan	65 198 888.35 (US$ 6 519 889)	5 688.56 (US$ 5 689)	912.42 (US$ 91.2)	1 898.12 (US$ 190)
External	739	47787.9	HK$	197 165 270.5 (US$ 25 342 578)	16 367.71 (US$ 2 104)	1 598.56 (US$ 205.5)	4 126.84 (US$ 530)

Exchange Rate in 1991 : US$1 : 10 Yuan, and US$1 : HK$7.78

Source : Shenzhen Real Estate Market Yearbook 1992

Table 5.3   Rental Index for Commodity Office Buildings in Shenzhen

Year	Luohu District		Futian District	
	Internal (Yuan)	External (HK$)	Internal (Yuan)	External (HK$)
1984	100	100	100	100
1985	117	109	133	110
1986	182	113	250	112
1987	251	128	346	121
1988	349	150	478	149
1989	478	165	666	256
1990	555	180	800	175
1991	716	239	818	230
Average price in 1991	5 270/sq.m or (US$ 527)	8 525/sq.m or (US$ 1 095)	4 200/sq.m or (US$ 420)	8 019/sq.m or (US$ 1 031)

Source : Shenzhen Real Estate Market Yearbook 1992

Table 5.4 compares the external market price of residential units with local residents' income and shows that it will be a long time before the strong investment in the external market can be absorbed by local users, and if the separation of markets continues, the external commodity housing market will become a pure investment market which will quickly reach its peak as prices have been rising rapidly in the past two years.

Table 5.4   Affordability Ratios for External Market Residential Units

Cities	(1) Property price US$/sq. ft	(2) Highest 15% local monthly income (US$)	(3) Mortgage payment (US$)	Affordability ratio % : (3) divided by (2)
Shenzhen	154	298.6	937	313
Guangzhou	103	268.8	624.7	232
Dongguan	45	268.8	273.3	101
Shanghai	128.5	268.8	780.8	290

Exchange rate is set at US$1 : HK$7.78

Source : HG Asia China Review, January 1993, Vol. 4, No. 1.

The Land Market

Pricing of Land in China under the Economic Reforms

Under the doctrine of socialism, land ownership has to remain with the State which represents the people. If land title cannot be sold or transferred there has to be a way to by-pass this limitation on the privatisation process. What the authorities in China have devised is the separation of land use rights from land ownership for a prescribed term (Walker, 1991). In April, 1987, the State Council proposed a new policy for the transferability of land use rights in the free market. The Special Economic Zones Office under the Council was delegated to test such idea in the four open areas of the nation, namely Tianjin, Shanghai, Guangzhou and Shenzhen.

Prior to the land use rights reforms, land had not been a tradable market commodity following the Chinese Communist Party's assumption of power in 1949. Therefore due to a lack of experience, some local authorities (with monopoly power over the sale of land use rights) failed to establish a basis of the measurement of land price when they were selling land use rights to foreign investors at the beginning of the land use rights reforms. This further motivated the state to speed up the establishment of guidelines for the local authorities as reference points in this very inefficient market.

One of the pioneer studies in this aspect was carried out in December 1985 by the Shanghai Urban Economics Society sponsored by the Shanghai City Planned Economy Research Institute. The researchers took 1161 samples from the major commercial land use zones (including general retailing, hardware, cigarette and candies, clothing, trading etc.), from which the average 3-yearly profit between 1982-1984 was obtained and then assuming a 12% average profit the differential profit was regressed. In 1988, a similar exercise was also carried out in Beijing. These pilot studies concentrated on the calculation of differential profits for different locations. This reflects the domination of the concept of differential rent from the Marxist interpretation of land rent (Marx,1981) in the establishment of a proxy for market land price at the beginning of the privatisation of land use rights in China, which illustrates that privatisation reforms in a socialist economic system will invariably involve the application of the existing concepts of land value consciously or unconsciously. The main reason is the easy reference and the politically feasible nature of these concepts. With this premise, the formulation of guidance land price can be examined in a more systematic manner through an interpretation of the extent to which the official view on land price behaviour under the privatisation of land use rights is affected by socialist concepts.

The Benchmark Pricing Model

Reforms in the real estate market are different from other price reforms in the consumer goods markets in China as prices existed in the consumer goods markets before any formal price reforms were undertaken. Allocation of such goods was based on the planned operation as well as the price mechanism, although in a very much subsidised and distorted way. In the real estate market however land had been allocated administratively, without charge, before the reforms. The conveyance and use of land were dealt with by means of application through administrative channels. Land was not required to be valued in monetary terms. After the LURs reforms, the establishment of an efficient price mechanism to allocate land resources among different users was therefore regarded of the utmost importance and urgency.

The opening up of the land market to investors created a need for the government to try to establish land prices in a market where there was virtually no comparison data available. The authorities came up with the idea that a market reference point of average land prices in each city should be complied so that the local authorities could have a set of guidelines when selling land to investors. This led to the formulation of the Benchmark Price (BMP) (Li,1995). This is the estimation (by a local authority) of land price on the basis of various land grades for different land uses in the city.

Benchmark prices are now established or are being established in various cities. The idea of this reference point appraisal system comes mainly from research by Hu (Hu,1990) who regards valuation as a means of control over the property market rather than as an appraisal of economic performance in the real estate market. Theoretically, assessment of land value is seen as a means to achieve three kinds of function:

- to control the real estate market through a price mechanism;
- to facilitate the transaction of LURs;
- to strengthen the management of the State's land resources.

According to Hu, the ideal determination process of land value comprises three stages of assessment:

- assessment of a BMP;
- assessment of a Land Transaction Base Price (LTBP);
- assessment of a Transaction Price (TP).

A BMP is the average price level established within a specific time period in a particular area/locality for a particular land use. It is set by the government land management departments and the state valuation committee according to transaction data as well as expected revenue from land (see Figure 5.1). Apart from being a baseline assessment of average land prices in a neighbourhood, it also provides a basis for the assessment of property taxes and capital gains tax similar to the function of the Announced Land Values in Taiwan for the assessment of capital gains tax of land by the government (Lin,1983). In addition, it provides a guideline for negotiation of land price when a specific site is about to be disposed of by the authority in a market where market comparables are hard to find.

Since the BMPs only give pictures of average land prices for different localities for reference purposes, a more specific land price determination mechanism is needed. The Land Transaction Base Price (LTBP) is the price level determined by each party when a LUR is to be sold, transferred or leased. It is estimated separately by both the land owner and land user (potential LUR buyer). They will base their valuations on such factors as supply of and demand for land and real property in the market, land revenue, planning regulations, location differences and the prevailing state land policies.

The LTBP is a reflection of each parties' separate idea of a hypothetical transaction price. Theoretically it reflects the quality of land management and income earning potential from that particular piece of land. It is based on the BMP. Unlike BMPs, it is determined by parties entering into a land sale contract who may be land management departments, valuation committees, real estate and housing departments, independent valuation agencies, banks, financial institutions as well as both parties. This is because the determination process is part of the market process which involves both the seller (the State) and the buyer (the investor).

Figure 5.1 Valuation Process of the Benchmark Prices in China

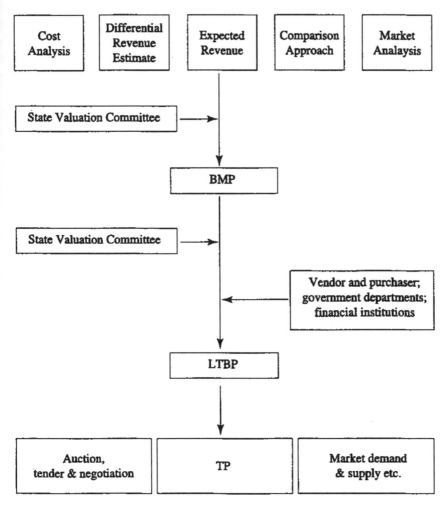

Source :   [Li, 1995].

When both parties have concluded their own valuations, they will negotiate and agree on a market land price by which the LUR is conveyed from the State to the investor. This is the Transaction Price (TP) which expresses the actual market exchange price level and forms the payment basis of the transaction. It establishes the price for a particular piece of land within a specific range of time and under the current market demand and supply policy and economic factors. After the transaction, the land management departments will register the TPs and take them into consideration when modifying BMPs in the future.

Figure 5.1 shows the various considerations that will be taken into account when assessing the BMPs. Cost analysis is the application of the cost approach to valuing land, which is currently still the predominant approach to valuation in China. Based on the profit earning potential of different enterprises and businesses on different sites, the differential revenue estimate mainly takes into account the effect of location on profitability of enterprises. Expected revenue in an urban context refers to the expected future revenue from the property development to be built on site. This is similar to the conventional income approach of valuation which equates land value with total expected future land income. Finally, in market analysis, market transaction prices are compared and considered and market demand and supply factors are analysed.

Benchmark Land Pricing Behaviour

The above outlines the theoretical measurement of BMPs for the determination of land price at the initial stage of the privatisation of land use rights in China. However the effectiveness of this appraisal process depends very much on how far this system reflects actual market activities. In theory, benchmark prices are relied on as a base from which local authorities can adjust prices according to the specific characteristics of the site being negotiated, assuming the benchmark prices established represent the general market demand and supply situation. The success of this official view of the guideline system depends very much how close this estimation is to the actual market situation.

In Shenzhen city for instance the BMPs appraisal process more or less follows the theoretical approach described above. Apart from grading land into different zones for the purpose of determining BMPs, the local authority also applies the so-called Delphi Analysis by which experts are called upon to rank these different zones under different criteria such as:

- Degree of prosperity;
- Town planning conditions;
- Physical and social infrastructure
- Amenities
- External communication
- Population density
- Internal transportation facilities
- Security in the neighbourhood
- Environment and natural conditions

From these analyses, Table 5.5 below shows the BMPs (for sale of land by private treaty) in the Shenzhen city for the year 1992. To allow for market changes, there is an allowance of 20% fluctuation or variance between any category in Use Type 1 in the same grade whilst a 10% fluctuation is allowed between any category in Use Type 2 in the same grade. This BMP table represents the reference points for land sales by private treaty only.

The practicality of the BMP rationale is challenged when compared with actual market transactions. Market land prices deviate substantially from the BMPs. For example, Table 5.6 shows the land sale in Shenzhen in 1991/92 by way of open tender (the grades to which these lots belong are not known). When comparing the magnitude of land prices in the two tables, it is not difficult to see that land prices achieved in the market under the open tender conveyance system are higher and in some cases substantially higher than the guideline land price. This substantial divergence in the figures from the two tables represents divergence in the market expectation of the potential of land from that of the local authority. One of the objectives of the formulation of the BMPs is to provide local authorities with a set of guidelines to determine a reasonable land price when negotiating with real estate developers for the conveyance of land use rights. The BMP table in this case does not provide a realistic reference which reflects the actual market demand and supply situation. Out of the fifteen land sales, only one piece of land has a price falling within the range covered by the BMP table. That means a number of market factors were excluded when the authority assessed the BMPs.

Furthermore, even if the BMPs are constantly updated by actual market transactions, there is also a problem of whether records of land sold by open tender or auction, or those of land sold under private treaty should be taken into consideration. This is because land prices achieved under these two different means of conveyance diverge quite substantially. Table 5.7

shows the difference between the average land prices when land is sold by private treaty and when sold by open tender in Shenzhen. It can be observed from Table 5.7 that selling land use rights through private treaty grant achieved a much lower market land price than by way of open tender where market competition existed. However, land prices achieved under private treaty grant approached the BMP in Shenzhen in 1992 (Table 5.5) much more than land prices achieved under open tender.

Table 5.5   Benchmark Price for Shenzhen City,
1992 (US$/sq.m.)

Grade / Use	Use Type 1	Use Type 2	Use Type 3	Use Type 4	Use Type 5
Grade 1	120	30	18	13	5
Grade 2	70	28	16	11	4
Grade 3	40	22	14	9	3
Grade 4	25	18	12	7	2
Grade 5	19	16	10	6	1

Use Type 1 : (Commercial, office, trading, services, finance, petrol filling station, high class residential villas, entertainment, etc)
Use Type 2 : (All kinds of residential properties except high class villas)
Use Type 3 : (All kinds of industries, warehouse, transportation facilities including ports, public utilities, etc)
Use Type 4 : (All kinds of open space area, including production area)
Use Type 5 : (Plantation, agricultural, animal rearing ground and tourist areas)

Exchange rate between US$ and Chinese Yuan before the introduction of the reform in exchange rate system on 1/1/1994 was US$1 : 10 Yuan).

Source : Shenzhen Economic Zone Legal Rules Compilation 1992.

**Table 5.6   Market Land Prices Achieved under Open Tender in
Shenzhen between 1991-92 (US$/sq.m.)**

Lot No. (Year)	Site area (sq. m)	Gross Floor Area (sq. m)	Price : US$/sq. m
B206-9 (1991)	13 576	18 200	62.61
B119-13 (1991)	5 146	26 000	301.205
B119-14 (1991)	7 274	12 600	261.204
B312-17 (1991)	5 000	10 000	300
B207-5 (1991)	9 336.7	14 600	285.968
B119-24 (1991)	3 579.6	14 800	502.849
B207-4 (1991)	11 042.3	15 800	253.57
B119-25 (1991)	3 579.6	14 800	502.849
B119-23 (1991)	3 975.8	14 800	503.043
B119-26 (1991)	3 975.8	14 800	503.043
B207-6 (1991)	11 858.1	35 600	324.251
B207-9 (1991)	7 694.3	9 235	212.561
B201-7 (1992)	5 460	-	1859
B201-9 (1992)	5 460	-	1811
B201-10 (1992)	5 460	-	1696

Exchange rate between US$ and Chinese Yuan before the introduction of the reform
in exchange rate system on 1/1/1994 was US$1 : 10 Yuan).

*Source : Li, G. Y. (1993) : Development and Investment of Real Estate in China,
Tianjin; Tianjin Technology Translation Publishing.*

Table 5.7　Price Differentials between Land Sold by Private Treaty and by Open Tender in Shenzhen from 1990 - 92 (US$/sq. m.)

	By Private Treaty	By Open Tender
1990	67	305
1991	76.9	491.1
1992 up to July	76.9	531.1

Exchange rate between US$ and Chinese Yuan in 1992 : US$1 : 10 Chinese Yuan.

Source : Chinese and Foreign Realestate Times 1992, issue 7, vol. 25.

This is a much more comprehensive application of benchmark pricing principles covering a very substantial area of the province. However, this only provides a very rough scale of the possible asking price. For instance, the benchmark price for grade one land for use type one (commercial) in Guangzhou and Shenzhen has a range of $US300/m² with an average price of $US550/m² (Table 5.8). This is about four times the average price for residential use in the same grade. However, when we look at property prices rather than land prices in this grade of land, the price differential is not so large. For instance, in Guangzhou, residential property prices in 1993 were about HK$6150/m² or $US790/m², while prices for commercial building were about HK$ 12800/m² or US$1645/m².

Such divergence between the land market and the property market is difficult to explain in terms of valuation theory. There is an obvious mismatch in the official view of market behaviour and the actual market expectation. This is probably a common problem in all immature and transitional economies. This transitional problem is also evident from the existence of the double-track land use system in China (Institute of Public Administration, 1991). This double-track system allows on one hand, the LURs to be sold in an open market system (which accounts for only a small portion of the land conversion process), and on the other allocated to various government institutions and state enterprises (running on a commercial basis) without payment of the land price even after the land use rights reforms have been initiated.

Table 5.8. Benchmark Price for Various Cities in Guangdong Province in 1993 (US$/sq. m.)

Grade	Location (Cities of Counties in Guangdong Province)	Commercial Use Type 1	Residential Use Type 2	Industrial Use Type 3
One	Guangzhou, Shenzhen	396 - 704	101.4 - 158.6	49.2 - 70.8
Two	Zhuhai, Shantou, Huizhou, Dongguan, Zhongshan, Foshan	313.9 - 546.1	82 - 127	45.6 - 64.3
Three	Jiangmen, Shunde, Pangyu, Baoan, Nanhai	236.8 - 403.2	58.4 - 87.6	42 - 58
Four	Yangjiang, Zhanjiang, Mouming, Zhaoqing, Chaozhou, Huaxian Sanshui	157.5 - 262.5	40.5 - 59.5	34 - 46
Five	Shaoguan, Heyuan, Zeizhou, Shanwei, Qingyuan, Huiyang, Doumen, Zengcheng, Taishan, Kaiping, Xinhui	98.8 - 161.2	29.5 - 42.5	25.8 - 34.2
Six	Puning, Chaoyang, Denghai, Nanao, Huidong, Songhua, Enping, Yunfu, Luoding, Gaoyao, Gaoming	69.3 - 110.7	22.4 - 31.6	20.9 - 21.7
Seven	Qujiang, Boluo, Chaoan, Haifeng, Lufeng, Wuchun, Dianbai, Huazhou, Sihui, Meixian, Yingde, Fugan	54.6 - 85.4	17.6 - 24.4	16.7 - 21.3
Eight	Gaozhou, Xuwen, Haikang, Qingjiang, Yangdong, Yangxi, Yangcun, Nongmen, Xingeng, Lechang, Qingxin, Lianxian	39.5 - 60.5	14.5 - 19.5	13.3 - 16.7
Nine	Xinyi, Fengkai, Deqing, Huaiji, Xinning, Lianping	32 - 48	12 - 16	10.8 - 13.2
Ten	Renhua, Shixing, Nanxioung, Wengyuan, Ruyan, Heping, Nongchun, Zijin, Luhe, Guangning, Dabu, Zhaoning, Pingyuan, Wuhua, Fengshun, Liamshan, Yangshan.	24.3 - 35.7	10.4 - 13.6	9.1 - 10.9

Exchange rate between US$ and Chinese Yuan before the introduction of the reform in exhange rate system on 1/1/1994 was US$1 : 10 Yuan.

Source : MingPao Daily 9/9/1993.

Therefore, assessing BMPs by examining the differential profits of the existing land users may distort the actual income earning potential of different sites as land users (such as state enterprises) who obtained land through the administrative channel may not carry out the economic activities that reflect the highest and best use of that site. Assessment of land price based on the information from these land users will therefore diverge from market expectations under the competitive environment towards which China is moving slowly, step by step.

Another unique characteristic of this State appraisal system is the fact that the nature of BMPs in China is always a component-structure rather than a single sum (Li,1995). This is not explicitly found in other economies such as the U.S.A. or the U.K For instance, the BMP table for Beijing city in 1993 is as shown in Table 5.9 from which the benchmark price for particular use (1) for a particular land grade is obtained by the following formula:

BMP/m^2 = (1) x PlotRatioFactor + [(2)+(3)] x PlotRatio + (4) x AdjustmentFactor + (5) or (6)

where:
- the adjustment factor is 2 when the sitting tenant to be resettled is a state enterprise, and 4 when it is a commercial or special land user;
- the plot ratio is the ratio of gross floor area to site area;
- the plot ratio factor is obtained from the following table;

plot ratio	1 or less	2	3	4	5	6	7	8	9	10
factor	1	1.91	2.74	3.5	4.2	4.9	5.6	6.3	7	7.7

For instance, an average site of grade one land for commercial use with plot ratio 7 where the existing tenant is a state enterprise has an average base land price of:

US$540 x 5.6 + [US$84 +US$35] x 7 + US$860 x 2 = US$ 5,577.00/m^2

In such cases, the average land price as appraised by the authority is composed of several elements. They are the price for the use rights of land,

Table 5.9   Benchmark Price for Beijing City in 1993 (US$/sq. m.)

Land Grade	Conveyance Fee				Infrastructure fee		Land Developpment fee		
	Com (1)	Apt (1)	Res (1)	Ind (1)	(2)	(3)	(4)	(5)	(6)
One	400 - 680	380 - 580	250 - 340	250 - 340	68 - 100	20 - 50	740 - 980	20 - 56	-
Two	300 - 400	280 - 380	200 - 250	200 - 250	68 - 100	20 - 50	740 - 980	20 - 56	-
Three	250 - 300	230 - 280	125 - 200	125 - 200	68 - 100	20 - 50	740 - 980	20 - 56	-
Four	190 - 250	180 - 230	100 - 125	100 - 125	68 - 100	20 - 50	740 - 980	20 - 56	-
Five	125 - 190	125 - 180	75 - 100	75 - 100	68 - 100	20 - 50	740 - 980	20 - 56	-
Six	65 - 125	65 - 125	50 - 75	50 - 75	68 - 100	20 - 50	740 - 980	20 - 56	10 - 23
Seven	50 - 65	40 - 65	20 - 50	20 - 50	68 - 100	20 - 50	740 - 98	20 - 56	10 - 23
Eight	10 - 50	10 - 40	8 - 20	8 - 20	68 - 100	20 - 50	-	-	10 - 23
Nine	8 - 10	5 - 10	4 - 8	4 - 8	68 - 100	20 - 50	-	-	10 - 23
Ten	5 - 8	4 - 5	3 - 4	3 - 4	68 - 100	20 - 50	-	-	10 - 23

Exchange rate between US$ and Chinese Yuan before the introduction of the reform in exchange rate system on 1/1/1994 was US$1 : 10 Yuan.

Where :

(1)   is the different land uses such as commercial, aartment, residential and industrial;
(2)   is the fee charged for urban services and the connection of public utilities e.g. gas etc;
(3)   is the fee charged for neighbourhood infrastructure;
(4)   is the resettlement fee in urban area;
(5)   is the resettlement fee in urban fringe area;
(6)   is the resettlement fee in rural area.

Source : Beijing City Government Document No. 34, 1993.

i.e., conveyance fee, payment for infrastructure development in the neighbourhood and compensation payment for sitting tenants. Such a definition of land price may be very different from that normally defined as an open market value in a market economy for which land price is normally represented by the discounted total future income obtainable from that particular site within town planning controls. The residual land value basis is the core to the determination of land price even when the authority buys back land from sitting tenants and resells it for development purposes (Needham,1992) as the deduction of residual land value would have taken preparation costs into consideration. The addition of the infrastructure development costs and the burden of resettlement to the land price shows that the Chinese authorities still view land price as a production cost such that land price is an additive element rather than a flow of future income.

To illustrate further the effect of the socialist objective theory of value on the privatisation process of land use rights in China, the pricing policy of State land in Hainan Province is examined. Under the ideological conception of the nature of land price developed by the benchmark pricing model as discussed previously, Haikou city, the capital of Hainan Province had their benchmark price table estimated and announced in mid-1993 as shown in Table 5.10.

This benchmark price is a baseline reference only. According to the local authority, the actual land price is composed of three elements:

LandPrice = BenchmarkPrice + PlotRatioLandPrice + FrontageLandPrice
where BenchmarkPrice is calculated as above;
PlotRatioLandPrice = BenchmarkPrice, if the plot ratio allowed is equal to 2.5
where it is higher, the plot ratio land price becomes:
BenchmarkPrice + (BenchmarkPrice/2.5) x 50% x Portion of PlotRatio above 2.5
Where it is smaller than 2.5, the plot ratio price is:
BenchmarkPrice - (BenchmarkPrice/2.5) x 25% x Portion of PlotRatio beneath 2.5
FrontageLandPrice = PlotRatioLandPrice x (site frontage x half of road width)

There are two observations from Table 5.10, the first is the difference in the compilation of the BMP from that of Shenzhen and Beijing, suggesting that the official view on land price behaviour varies between local authorities.

Table 5.10 Benchmark Price for Haikou City, Capital of Hainan Province in 1993 (US$/sq. m.)

Location Type	Land Grade	Total Land Price	Convey Fee of Land	Cost Portion (1)	(2)	(3)	(4)	(5)	(6)	(7)	(8)
A	One	120	0.2	0.1	1	4.8	10	10	15	3	75.9
	Two	75	0.2	0.1	1	4.8	10	10	15	3	30.9
	Three	60	0.2	0.1	1	4.8	10	10	15	3	15.9
B	One	75	0.2	0.1	1	4.8	10	10	7.5	3	38.4
	Two	60	0.2	0.1	1	4.8	10	10	7.5	3	23.4
	Three	45	0.2	0.1	1	4.8	10	10	7.5	3	8.4
C	One	60	0.2	0.1	1	4.8	10	10	7.5	3	27.9
	Two	45	0.2	0.1	1	4.8	10	10	7.5	3	12.9

Exchange rate between US$ and Chinese Yuan before the introduction of the reform in exhange rate system on 1/1/1994 was US$1 : 10 Yuan.

The benchmark price of land for a particular grade in a particular location type is the conveyance fee of land plus (1) to (8)

Where:
(1) is the land management fee;
(2) is the agricultural land tax;
(3) is the vegetable land development fund;
(4) is the land acquisition compensation;
(5) is the neighbourhood infrastructure fee;
(6) is the city construction fee;
(7) is the urban services and infrastructure fee;
(8) is the resettlement of sitting tenants fee.

Source : Chinese and Foreigh Real Estate Times, Issue 1, 1993.

The second is that once again there is a strong preference for looking at land price as a component structure consisting of various costs for preparing site for development.

What is suggested by the BMP compilation in practice is that the production cost function of development land plays a major role in the determination of land price in China. This contradicts the established concept that value is not equal to cost.

Conclusion

A guideline system is certainly needed in such a large market as China in terms of geographical size and capital value as the one in China. Such a concept is especially important in a market where there is no track record of market activities. The idea of setting a baseline land price for reference in a transitional land market of which the existing Chinese government had no experience is useful and logical for better control of the market.

What the BMP concept proposes is a theoretical and idealistic approach that the State can provide baseline land prices on the basis of which the privatisation of market operations can be carried out more easily. The three levels of the appraisal process described provide a consistent and coherent relationship between the government's effort in monitoring the market and the actual market performance. To turn the BMPs from being a baseline reference into a more representative analysis of the actual market more frequent updates of the BMP tables by market data is needed. This is not easy given the lack of a relatively efficient real estate market in China. Even if this was done there remains the problem of which market transactions should be included. The divergence in land prices achieved under different land sale procedures reflects the immaturity and inefficiency of the market. In any case, land price should reflect the future cash flow pattern of the particular site, even in a market where few comparables exist. Keith (Keith,1991) comments that discounted cash flow analysis may be one of the best techniques for appraising non-agricultural tracts in transition when few comparable sales exist.

As noted, it is certainly logical and reasonable for the Chinese authorities to establish their official view on land price behaviour at the beginning of the privatisation of land use rights as there is no market information for them to work on. Since the release of land use rights is monopolised by the State in China, it is very important for the authority to understand the nature of market land price in the transition period in order to establish a more efficient market.

The deviation between BMP in theory and practice exhibits the fact that market land price behaviour is not yet regarded as a reasonable model by the Chinese authorities. It is however not the authorities' ignorance of the market mechanism that causes this deviation. It is the politically most convenient view on land price behaviour that causes the differences. The pricing of land in a component-structure is due to many reasons.

One is the difficulties which may be encountered by the State in resettling sitting tenants who are enjoying the virtual freehold interest under the old land use allocation system without a properly registered property right. In such cases, the authorities can seek from the developer a sum that is just enough for the transfer of the encumbered freehold interest and resettle the tenants themselves or the authorities can let the developer deal with the negotiation of resettlement. Either way the authorities find it less troublesome than charging the developer the full residual land value. In addition, the possible problem of the need for profit sharing in terms of land revenue with the central government may also discourage the local governments from recovering full residual land value.

The pricing behaviour of the BMP for various cities in China has been examined from both a theoretical viewpoint and at the practical implementation level. The idea of BMP of land use rights in China is to set up a guideline for a smooth transition into a market mechanism for land. What is being devised in various cities however follows very much the same ideological path as the socialist conception of value, or the production cost function basis of value.

This is not difficult to understand given the blurred property rights in China and the extensive disregard of price mechanism in the allocation of land since 1949. Interestingly enough, this seems to be the easiest way out for the privatisation of land in such a huge transitional economy as no market comparables will be available for a more proper pricing model to be set up before the market generates enough activities.

6 The Impact of China's Economic Reforms upon the Construction Industry

The construction industry is playing a leading role in China's rapid economic expansion. There can be no economic activity without construction. The increase in economic activity has generated, and will continue to do so, a heavy demand for construction. This chapter assesses the impact of the economic reforms upon the construction industry.

Constraints on the Growth

Domestic infrastructure bottlenecks are clearly beginning to constrain the rate of growth. The rapid growth since 1991 has increased the pressure on already strained transport and energy supplies. Anecdotal evidence suggests that China's transport infrastructure is stretched to its limit and is falling behind the pace of demand growth. In 1992, recorded freight transportation overall grew only 3.8% (in terms of tons per km) over the year, with highway freight transport growing a mere 2% and railway freight transport being able to accommodate only a 5.9% increase over the year (Harrold,1993). Railways are a major part of the transportation system in China. As most industries and mines are located in the east, the system that serves the eastern half of the country is heavily overburdened. It is estimated that the railway network is able to cope with only 60% of current demand for rail transport services (EIU,1994). This bottleneck also obliges China to import grain for the cities on the eastern seaboard, even though China is able to produce most of the grain needed. The technological level of the service, including traction, rolling stock, telecommunication and signalling, is mostly outdated. As far as the situation of the country's ports is concerned, it seems that average ship turnaround times have increased significantly. In 1992 more than 50% of ships arriving in port at any given time had to wait before they could be handled (Harrold,1993).

Likewise there is growing evidence of energy shortages in the coastal provinces, where, it is estimated, energy supply is currently meeting only

75% of demand (Harrold,1993). Energy shortages force factories to run well below capacity. For instance, even in the SEZs in relatively developed south China, only four to five days of normal electricity supply can be guaranteed (Chen,1993). In the case of the Hainan SEZ, some factories are forced to stop production for three days each week because of energy shortages (Chen,1993). The coal output is predicted to lag behind domestic demand by 120 million tons by the end of the century and the technological level is believed to be more than a decade behind that of developed countries (EIU,1994).

Office blocks and residential houses are extremely crowded in China. Many small companies have to rent a room in a hotel as their office. Families with children living in just one bedroom are common in the big cities like Shanghai. Telecommunications are also under development especially for domestic use. In 1991 there was only one telephone for every 77 people (Harrold,1993).

The deprivations of the Cultural Revolution have left China desperately short of technical skills. The Cultural Revolution disrupted the country's education system during 1966-77, when almost all the higher education institutions experienced enormous difficulties. Furthermore, the economic reforms and the introduced responsibility system, particularly in the agriculture communities, gave people an incentive to work in the fields instead of going to school or university. The charges made to fund teachers' pay also encouraged people to stay away from school. Therefore, China has suffered, and will continue for many years to suffer, from an acute shortage of skilled personnel, especially at middle management level. For instance, local management staff in many joint ventures have been found to be insufficiently educated to adapt to environmental change and absorb new concepts, and need further substantial training (Chen,1993).

Construction and Investment

The aim of creating a heavy industrial base has dominated investment patterns since 1949 and the investment ratio has typically been over 30% of national income (SSBC,1993). Large-scale projects such as hydroelectricity and water control, bridge building and the construction of factory plant in the heavy industry sector took priority over housing and small-scale investment. The concept of 'non-productive construction' as an element of capital construction indicates the manner in which the perceived need to increase productive capacity has dominated planners' minds in the face of shortages of funds and materials. The latter has slowed the rate of completion and the poor quality of many construction materials has produced a quaint official statistic - the good quality rate of projects undertaken by State-owned construction enterprises, which remained static at 58% between 1981 and 1988, but fell to 41.5% in 1991 (SSBC,1993). There are around 6.4 million workers in State-owned construction units (SSBC,1993).

In order to meet the new demands of fast growth, China has recognised it must change many of its approaches. It has called for a reform of the industry focusing on quicker construction times, improved quality, increased returns on investment, and the introduction of a public tendering system. The changes have had three significant impacts on the construction market.

First, the greater freedom given to enterprises to make investment decisions and raise funds has led to a boom in extra-budgetary (i.e. not provided for in the annual budget) investment, much of it in residential units for workers, office blocks and hotels. Only 10% of capital construction was extra-budgetary in 1953-57, but this share rose to 23% in 1976-80 and reached a colossal 93.2% in 1991, funded largely by self-generated funds, domestic borrowing and foreign investment (SSBC,1993). The resulting increase in demand for construction work has produced shortages of building materials and generated higher prices, and the government is again making efforts to restrict such construction. Access to loans for construction projects has been made more difficult and banks have been instructed to call in loans destined for purely speculative property investments. Non-productive projects outside the state plan are subject to a special 30% tax and were in practice banned in the 1988 and 1993 austerity programmes.

Second, FDI with the majority of joint ventures has been increasing. It is still a relatively small proportion of the total capital construction but represents a large market in absolute terms. In 1991 the value of FDI in construction was US$5.9 billion, accounting for 5.7% of the total capital construction in the country over that year (EIU,1994).

Third, a system whereby new projects must be put out to competitive tender among construction companies has been devised with an attempt to make construction generally more efficient and less liable to cost overrun. To a western contractor, competitive tendering may not seem a major step, but Chinese contractors have been used to projects being allocated to them.

In addition, the number of new state projects under the annual plans was held down in the 1991-95 plan, with priority given to 'key construction projects', mainly in energy, transport, telecommunications and the provision of extra capacity to produce raw and semi-finished materials. Strict instructions were given forbidding undertaking construction projects when problems can be solved by technological transformation, renovation or expansion of existing facilities. Despite these moves, total investment in fixed assets rose by an average of 26% a year in current prices between 1983 and 1988, over double the rate of increase in national income, and after a fall of 7% in 1989 rebounded to 7.6% growth in 1990, 18.6% in 1991 and 37.6% in 1992 (SSBC,1993). In 1993 investment in fixed assets rose more than 60% over the same period in the previous year (SSBC,1994).

Construction and the National Economy

The construction industry in China was not recognised officially as a separate industry until 1983. In the past, it was viewed as a subordinate part of government investment. Therefore, the construction industry was regarded as producing no financial value through design and construction activities. The creative contribution of construction industry to the national economy was denied.

In fact, the construction industry plays a very important role in the national economy. The share of construction output in GNP has increased from 13.9% in 1988 to 23.7% in 1994, reaching RMB975 billion (US$112 billion). In 1992, the construction industry employed a total of 19.6 million people, about 10% of the total employment of the country, excluding the individual labour in cities, towns and rural areas (Table 6.1).

In respect of construction enterprises, the number of enterprises in 1992 was 77,857, an increase of 6.5% when compared with the figure in 1991 (Table 6.2). The State-owned enterprises accounted for just 6.4% of this total number (urban collective-owned and rural units accounted for 12.3% and 81.3% respectively), although 34.7% of the workforce were employed by the State-owned units (urban collective-owned and rural units employed 24.5% and 40.8%). In terms of output value, the State-owned enterprises contributed 43.4% of the total construction output in the country, although their number only accounted 6.4% of the total number of enterprises. This indicates that the State-owned construction enterprises usually had much larger scale projects in terms of production and employment than other types of construction companies.

Table 6.1   China: Construction Industry

	1988	1989	1990	1991	1992	1993	1994
% of construction output in GNP	13.9	18.4	16.7	16.1	20.7	24.5	23.7
Gross fixed asset investment (Rmb bn; current prices)	449.7	413.8	444.9	550.9	785.5	1245.8	1593.0
Real change of gross fixed asset investment (%)	15.5	0.2	-1.3	6.5	25.0	27.0	18.0
Capital construction investment * (Rmb bn; current prices)	-	-	170.4	211.6	301.3	464.7	628.7
Real change of capital construction investment (%)	-	-	12.3	21.8	37.6	54.2	35.3
Government's expenditure on capital construction (Rmb bn; current prices)	-	62.6	72.6	74.0	76.5	90.1	79.5e
% of government capital construction expenditure in the total government expenditure	-	20.6	21.0	19.4	17.4	17.0	13.1
Value-added of construction industry (Rmb bn; current prices)	-	-	-	-	139	211	290
Real change of value-added of construction industry (%)	-	-	-	-	18	15	12
Number of construction enterprises	87 224	80 106	74 145	73 094	77 857	-	-
Employment by construction enterprises (m)	19.0	17.7	17.2	17.8	19.6	-	-

e : EIU estimates; * : Capital construction investment of state-owned units only.

Sources :   *China : Country Report, 1993, 1994, 1995, The Economist Intelligence Unit (EIU);*
China : Country Forecast, 1995, The Economist Intelligence Unit (EIU); China
Statistical Year Book, 1992, 1993, 1994, State Statistical Bureau of PRC; The
Economist, August 1995; Statistical Communiqué of the State Statistical Bureau
of the PRC on the National Economic and Social Development 1990 - 94.

Table 6.2 also shows some economic indicators of the construction enterprises. The floor space of buildings under construction and completed in 1992 was 58 7 million m² and 281 million m², which represented an annual growth rate over 1991 of 25% and 23% respectively. The better completion rate of urban collective-owned enterprises shows their productivity is generally higher than that of State-owned enterprises. Moreover, there was a 61% increase in the total profit in 1992. Again, the ratio of profit rate/gross output of the urban collective-owned units (2.8% in 1992) was higher than that of the State-owned enterprises (1.8% in 1992), which reflects the better production performance of the urban collective-owned enterprises.

The major sources of finance were self-raised funds (over 60%) and domestic loans (over 20%) as shown in Table 6.3. The financial support direct from the central government had dramatically decreased, from 8.2% of the State budget in 1989 to only 3.7% in 1993. Meanwhile, the role of foreign investment has increased. Its share in the total investment in assets amounted to 7.3% in 1993, larger than that of the State budget. Table 6.3 also shows that more than 60% of construction investment went to the productive construction sector including factor building and infrastructure industry. Only about 30% of the construction investment went to non-productive construction, such as residential housing. Around 70% of the total construction investment went to State-owned enterprises. However, the gross output value of State-owned enterprises was only around 40% and their total profits were almost the same as that of the urban collective-owned enterprises (Table 6.2). This indicates that the State-owned enterprises were much less efficient than the urban collective-owned enterprises and rural construction teams.

Table 6.4 shows that the gross fixed asset investment of construction in 1992 was RMB785.5 billion, in which Guangdong province was the region with the greatest investment and represented 12% of the total construction investment in the country.

The average scale of State-owned enterprises was larger than other forms of enterprises not only in terms of the amount of investment but also in terms of employment. As shown in Table 6.5, there were 4,985 State-owned enterprises employing 6.8 million people, and 9,551 collective-owned enterprises employing 4.8 million people. This indicates that the average employment of each State-owned enterprise was 1,366 persons, while this figure in the collective-owned enterprise was only 499 persons.

Table 6.2   Distributions of Major Indicators of Construction Enterprises

	Total	State-owned units	Urban collective-owned units	Rural construction teams
Number of enterprises				
1988	87 224 (100%)	3 798 (4.4%)	10 336 (11.8%)	73 090 (83.8%)
1989	80 106 (100%)	3 927 (4.9%)	9 179 (11.5%)	67 000 (83.6%)
1990	74 145 (100%)	4 275 (5.8%)	9 052 (12.2%)	60 818 (82.0%)
1991	73 094 (100%)	4 638 (6.3%)	9 187 (12.6%)	59 269 (81.1%)
1992	77 857 (100%)	4 985 (6.4%)	9 551 (12.3%)	63 321 (81.3%)
Employment (m)				
1988	19.0 (100%)	6.2 (32.8%)	4.2 (22.1%)	8.6 (45.1%)
1989	17.7 (100%)	6.1 (34.5%)	3.9 (22.0%)	7.7 (43.5%)
1990	17.2 (100%)	6.2 (36.0%)	3.9 (22.7%)	7.1 (41.3%)
1991	17.8 (100%)	6.4 (36.0%)	4.2 (23.6%)	7.2 (40.4%)
1992	19.6 (100%)	6.8 (34.7%)	4.8 (24.5%)	8.0 (40.8%)
Gross output value (Rmb bn; current prices)				
1988	195.9 (100%)	77.7 (39.7%)	35.5 (18.1%)	82.7 (42.4%)
1989	216.9 (100%)	87.9 (40.5%)	40.4 (18.6%)	88.6 (40.4%)
1990	194.8 (100%)	93.5 (48.0%)	41.0 (21.0%)	60.3 (31.5%)
1991	228.5 (100%)	106.2 (46.5%)	50.2 (22.0%)	72.1 (31.5%)
1992	329.9 (100%)	143.2 (43.4%)	74.2 (22.5%)	12.5 (34.1%)

Continued

Table 6.2   Distributions of Major Indicators of Construction Enterprises   *Continued*

	Total	State-owned units	Urban collective-owned units	Rural construction teams
Floor space of building (million. m²)				
Under construction				
1991	--	272.6.0	196.6	--
1992	--	327.1.0	259.9	--
Completed				
1991	--	126.0	106.9	--
1992	--	151.3	130.0	--
Completion rate (%)				
1991	--	46.2	54.4	--
1992	--	46.3	50.0	--
Total profit (Rmb bn; current prices)				
1991	--	1.59	1.26	--
1992	--	2.55	2.05	--
Profit rate / Gross output (%)				
1991	--	1.5	2.5	--
1992	--	1.8	2.8	--

Sources : China Statistical Year Book 1993, State Statistical Bureau of PRC.

Table 6.3　Distribution of Gross Fixed Asset Investment by Source, Purpose and Type of Enterprise (%)

	1989	1990	1991	1992	1993	1994
Total Investment in assets	100.0	100.0	100.0	100.0	100.0	--
By source of funds						
State budget	8.2	8.7	6.8	4.3	3.7	--
Domestic loans	17.3	19.6	23.5	27.4	23.5	--
Foreign investment	6.6	6.2	5.7	5.8	7.3	--
Self-generated funds	67.9	65.5	64.0	62.5	65.5	--
By purpose						
Productive construction	62.2	62.2	62.7	65.8	--	--
Non-productive construction	37.8	37.8	37.3	34.1	--	--
(of which : residential)	(67.9)	(84.4)	(70.0)	(63.9)	--	--
By type of enterprise						
State-owned units	--	65.8	67.4	67.3	70.3	71.3
Collectively-owned units	--	12.4	11.9	16.3	17.7	17.3
Individuals	--	21.8	20.7	16.4	12.0	11.4

Sources : China : Country Report, 1993, 1994, 1995, The Economist Intelligence Unit (EIU); China Statistical Year Book 1992, 1993, 1994, State Statistical Bureau of PRC.

Table 6.4   Distribution of Gross Fixed Asset Investment by Purpose, Type of Enterprise and Selected Region, 1992 (Rmb bn; current prices)

Region	Total	Productive construction				Non-productive construction			
		Sub-total	State-owned units	Collective-owned units	Individuals	Sub-total	State-owned units	Collective-owned units	Individuals
National total	785.5	516.6	368.8	116.7	31.1	268.9	158.5	19.2	91.1
Beijing	26.3	13.7	11.3	2.2	0.2	12.6	11.5	0.5	0.7
Guangdong	93.9	60.0	38.3	17.0	4.7	33.9	21.8	3.4	8.7
Liaoning	43.1	28.2	24.1	3.3	0.8	14.9	12.0	0.7	2.3
Shandong	59.8	42.9	24.7	16.2	2.0	16.8	9.6	2.2	5.1
Shanghai	35.6	24.0	18.2	5.5	0.1	11.8	9.4	0.7	1.8
Sichuan	40.2	25.5	19.7	3.9	1.9	14.6	8.4	1.0	5.3
Zhejiang	44.4	26.4	10.5	12.6	3.3	19.0	5.0	1.5	5.3

Sources : China Statistical Year Book 1993, State Statistical Bureau of PRC.

Table 6.5   Number of Construction Enterprises and Employment by Type of Enterprise and Region, 1992

		Productive construction	Productive construction
State-owned units	National total	4 985	6 812
	Beijing	91	298.6
	Guangdong	239	268.7
	Liaoning	434	272.1
	Shandong	283	356.9
	Shanghai	85	117.8
	Sichuan	80	188.2
	Zhejiang	335	350.8
Collective-owned units	National total	9 551	4 763
	Beijing	59	240.0
	Guangdong	632	492.1
	Liaoning	967	265.8
	Shandong	1 312	587.9
	Shanghai	227	198.5
	Sichuan	59	130.8
	Zhejiang	946	341.5

Source :   China Statistical Year Book 1993, State Statistical Bureau of PRC.

Table 6.6 shows that the largest construction output in 1993 was from the civil engineering sector (87.5%), of which Guangdong province contributed the largest share of 15%. These civil engineering productions reflected the development of the economic zones and the improvement of infrastructure in the region. The output of construction installation work was 10.4% of the total construction output in 1993, standing in second place. Northern China, especially Liaoning province undertook the largest amount of work in the fields of construction installation, building repair and maintenance and non-standard equipment manufacture.

Furthermore, during the period of 1985-1992, the major types of construction works were new construction and expansion. The construction investment of State-owned enterprises on the new construction and expansion was RMB149 billion and RMB100 billion respectively in 1992 (Table 6.7). The major construction investments of State-owned enterprises were heavy industry (mainly the energy industry) and transport and telecommunication sectors (Table 6.7).

Types of Construction Companies

In the past, most construction companies in China were State-owned. Since China adopted the open door policy, other types of construction companies are growing more popular and are playing a more important role and the Chinese government has actively encouraged the establishment of other types of construction companies. The main reason is that it can provide more economic benefit to society. In addition, they are not burdened with large numbers of staff as most state-owned companies have to do.

Table 6.6   Distribution of Construction Output by Sector and Region, 1993 (%)

	Total	Civil Engineering	Construction installation	Building repair & maintenance	Non-standard equipment manufacture
National total	100	87.5	10.4	1.4	0.7
Beijing	6.5	6.5	5.0	14.3	2.1
Guangdong	14.0	15.0	6.8	8.7	3.5
Jiangsu	6.0	5.9	7.1	4.7	4.6
Liaoning	9.8	9.2	12.8	22.3	18.6
Shanghai	3.1	2.8	5.6	1.7	3.9
Sichuan	6.3	6.4	5.3	4.7	6.2
Tianjin	1.9	1.9	1.5	1.4	2.5
Zhejiang	3.8	3.9	3.6	3.9	3.8

Source :   China Statistical Year Book 1993, State Statistical Bureau of PRC.

**Table 6.7   Capital Construction Investment of State-owned Units
(Rmb bn; current prices)**

	1985	1990	1991	1992
Total investment	107.4	170.4	211.6	301.3
By source of funds				
State budget	38.1	36.4	34.8	30.8
Domestic loans	18.8	37.9	52.7	83.1
Foreign investment	7.4	22.4	24.0	33.4
Self-generated funds	34.0	53.0	74.7	124.3
Others	9.2	20.8	25.4	29.6
By purpose				
Productive construction	61.1	123.6	151.0	211.8
Non-productive construction	46.3	46.8	60.5	89.5
(of which residential)	(21.5)	(17.0)	(23.6)	(32.7)
By type of construction				
New construction	48.1	82.3	98.3	148.5
Expansion	35.0	61.1	77.9	100.3
Replacement	17.2	17.5	23.0	35.1
By Sector				
Agriculture	3.6	6.7	8.6	11.3
Industry	44.6	95.3	114.7	145.8
Light industry	6.3	12.2	15.2	21.7
Heavy industry	38.3	83.1	99.5	124.1
(Energy industry)	(20.5)	(55.8)	(64.6)	(80.4)
Transport, postal & telecommunication	17.1	20.7	33.1	44.8

Source :   China Statistical Year Book 1993, State Statistical Bureau of PRC.

Briefly, most of the construction companies act as general or main contractors and others as specialist trade contractors. The types of past ownership of construction companies in China include the following:

- State-owned units under the State Budget. These companies are under the direct management and financial control of the government. They may be owned by ministries.
- Collective-owned units not under the State Budget but owned by the people as a whole (in reality owned by the State). For example, the provinces, municipalities and cities have local construction corporations which report directly to the local construction commission. While a construction corporation oversees a number of construction companies within its municipality and is responsible for different building associated organisations.
- True collective-owned units through rural construction teams. The means of production are collectively owned by the workers, they can be run by villages, cities, towns and neighbourhood committees.

Whereas the newer types of ownership for the construction companies are listed as follows:

- individual owned units refer to the businesses which are owned by individuals.
- joint ownership units refer to the businesses which are capitalised by both foreign and domestic companies.
- wholly-owned foreign units refer to the businesses which are owned by foreign investors including overseas Chinese.

Since China is under transition from the old system to the new system, many things are undergoing rapid change. To cope with these changes, a type of ownership has been developed which is the share holding sector. It is a relatively new business in China and so there are only a small number of cases of this type. It refers to the business where the registered capital is from share holders. All the share holders jointly own the business. The shares of these companies are available in the share market in big cities, such as Shanghai and Shenzhen. Some can even be purchased in the overseas share markets.

In addition, there are a large number of design institutes which are mostly owned by the State. Since there is a law that the design of major projects should be practically undertaken and approved by the State-owned design institutes, very few private or collective design offices have been found around the country. Apart from the construction companies, there are a great number of consultancy companies for construction supervision. Some short-term courses for engineers on construction supervision are provided in some institutes or universities, such as the Shenzhen University. Hence, more people can then be qualified to supervise the work for social benefit purpose.

Problems in the Construction Industry

Although the construction industry in China has developed very fast and has made significant contributions to the national economy, there are still many problems existing in this sector.

Severe Distortion in the Pricing Mechanism

Under the planned economy, the construction projects were allocated to construction enterprises by the authorities at different levels, rather than through competitive tendering. The costs of construction projects were calculated from quantities of work and norms, the latter were yardsticks for labour, material and plant consumption. These norms were worked out by the local authorities in a unified manner and were controlled by the central government. These criteria are still used in pricing building and installation work for domestic projects even when a tendering procedure has been adopted.

Due to the insufficiency of the legal system and the complex administration procedures, the progress of the reform of the construction price mechanism has been very slow. The contradiction between 'stagnant norms' and the 'dynamic actual costs' of construction projects has led to many problems regarding tendering, payment, contract management and performance.

For instance, under the unified cost estimation system, the profit rate of any building or installation work was fixed at 4%. Furthermore, the excessive reduction of the contract price imposed by the client upon the contractor during contract negotiation has often made the actual profit rate lower than 3% because of the competition in the contracting market. Meanwhile, the market prices of labour, materials and machine costs have been increasing rapidly. Therefore, many contracting companies suffer from large financial losses. This phenomenon becomes even more severe for less standard or routine construction projects (Lu,1994).

The Underdeveloped Construction Market

The co-existence of the central-planned economy and the market economy leads to a construction market in chaotic order to a certain degree. With intervention from central and local government, most clients have not become a real prevailing party in the construction market. Many construction projects have not been put into the tendering market. The client, sometimes, does not have the authority to complete and maintain his project as required in the contact. There is a lack of consultancy companies to provide services, such as feasibility studies, design, preparation of tender documents, assessment of tenders, construction supervision, training of skilled personnel. Building materials and financial sources are very limited. The legal system is incomplete and is at the infant stage. There is a lack of law and regulation to assure the all the parties observe their obligations and obtain their rights.

The Lack of Initiative of the State-owned Construction Companies

The iron bowl philosophy still remains in the structure and operation mechanism of large and medium-sized State-owned construction companies. These companies usually have the advantages over collective-owned and individual unit companies in terms of experience, technology and constructional plant. In order to get support from the central and local government, they have to obey the directive or orders from the authorities at different level. They had plenty of works to erect in the past, however, due to their rigid operation policy and lack of flexible strategy to meet the challenge of the competitive contracting market, they are failing to obtain new contracts through the tendering procedure.

Conclusion

This chapter has presented some of the impacts of the economic reforms upon the construction industry. Although the construction industry has developed very fast, problems still remain which are caused by the built-in defects of the central-planned economy system.

This chapter has also shown that the heavy demand for construction caused by the rapid economic growth cannot be satisfied by China's prevailing resources either physical, technological or managerial. The construction industry in China has suffered for many years as a result of long construction cycles, inadequate planning and programming of projects and poor quality of workmanship. Therefore an increasing number of construction projects are promoted for international tendering. From that, not only can advanced technology be introduced, but also advanced management practices be imported. This huge emerging construction market has attracted world-wide interest.

7 Foreign Investment in the Construction Industry

The increase in China's economic activity has generated, and will continue to do so, a heavy demand for construction; a demand that cannot be satisfied by China's prevailing resources either physical, technological or managerial. This huge emerging Chinese construction market has attracted the interest of consultants and contractors world wide. The construction industry in China has suffered for many years as a result of long construction cycles, inadequate planning and programming of projects and poor quality of workmanship. Therefore an increasing number of construction projects are promoted for international tendering. From that, not only can advanced technology be introduced, but also advanced management practices can be imported.

This chapter summarises the construction demand in China and explores the consequent opportunities for foreign construction companies. It also analyses foreign participation and the problems encountered in the Chinese market, and finally, makes recommendations on future co-operation between the Chinese and foreign contractors.

Construction Demand

The construction industry has ambitious targets to meet by the year 2000. The main areas where construction is continuing to increase substantially in China are: infrastructure, rural and urban housing and tourism. Most of the key construction projects, which involve infrastructure construction, are located either in the major cities along the east coast or in the inland cities because of the importance in transport and resource development. Another important kind of construction activity involves property development such as rural and urban housing which was formerly principally located only in the Special Economic Zones but is now spreading into the coastal areas. The source of information used in this section is mainly from (EIU,1993).

Power Generation

Hydroelectricity Hydroelectricity will be the key area of growth and Western private capital and World Bank assistance are expected in the development. The largest currently operating station is at Gezhouba (the Three Gorges) on the Yangtse river, with a capacity of about 2,700 mw. Flooding in 1991 gave new impetus to the long debated and highly controversial plan to build the world's largest dam and hydroelectric station at the scenic Three Gorges area of the Yangtse river. The scheme will have a capacity of 17,000 mw of electricity and would bring large benefits in flood control and navigation. Most of the hydro potential is located away from the main industrial centres, necessitating heavy investment in transmission lines and systems.

Nuclear Plant Developing nuclear energy is also prominent. The first nuclear power plant, using a Chinese-designed 300 mw pressurised water reactor, at Qinshan in Zhejiang, was commissioned in 1992. A second phase to add 1,200 mw is planned. Construction of a similar reactor (a 900 mw plant, later to be doubled to 1,800 mw) at Daya Bay in Guangdong province has been completed recently. A further 2,400 mw plant is also planned for Guangdong and assistance from Western companies is sought.

Energy Development Foreign investment has been sought to develop coal mining. Major investment is planned which, together with imported plant and technology, is aimed to bring about the required expansion in generating capacity. For example, an agreement for the planning and design of coal projects was signed with the US company, Bechtel, originally involving the expenditure of US$600 million by Occidental, and is in operation at the Antaibao mine at Pingshuo in Shandong province.

Transport

Railway and Road As far as railway transportation is concerned, extension, further electrification and double tracking the system are investment priorities, including a new north-south link connecting Beijing and Guangdong, bisecting the existing coastal (via Shanghai) and central (via Wuhan) routes. Foreign technology and consultancy services are sought. The growth in border trade makes the expansion of rail lines even more pressing, and the improvement in relations with Vietnam has led to reconstruction work on the rail link between Hanoi and Nanning in Guangdong province.

Several major expressways, such as the Guangzhou-Shenzhen-Zhuhai expressway which involves 240 kilometres of road with a bridge at the mouth of the Zhujiang river, are also under construction.

Port and Airport Because the major river systems flow west to east, north to south traffic has been limited in the past, but as part of the modernisation programme China has an ambitious plan to link the five major waterways — the Yangtse, Pearl, Huai, Yellow and Han rivers — which, in turn, will be linked with the expansion of major ports. A major investment programme is under way to improve facilities at the principal coastal ports of Qinhuangdao, Tianjin and Shanghai and new harbours for ocean-going vessels will be built in various other coastal cities in anticipation of the opening of direct shipping links with Taiwan. Besides the main airports in Beijing, Shanghai and Guangzhou, other major cities in the eastern coastal areas and the inland such as Tianjin, Urumqi, Kunming, Harbin are also expanding both domestic and international airports.

Telecommunication

As part of the modernisation drive, priority has also been given to expanding and renovating the telecommunication system. The Chinese hope to replace urban crossbar switching with stored programme control systems in the near future. The Chinese government also announced in 1995 an end to the phone monopoly. Private investment and foreign investment are being encouraged to establish telephone network and run services

Commercial and Residential Buildings

Hotel and Office buildings Tourist arrivals have been increasing greatly. China has opened more than 150 cities to overseas visitors. In 1992, there were 45 million foreign tourists visiting China (SSBC,1993). International standard hotels have sprung up in major cities, many with foreign equity participant and management. Furthermore, many foreign contractors have been involved in interior decoration for major hotels and restaurants, because the general finishing work undertaken by the Chinese companies cannot meet international standards.

Unlike most Western countries, commercial buildings are not very common in China. Most foreign companies set up their offices in hotel rooms. However, as China's outside contacts grow and more people are coming to China for business, the need for office space is increasing. Therefore, office buildings are the major construction projects for foreign contractors as those projects usually require advanced techniques, such as construction of curtain walls and structural steel frames with which China's construction enterprises are not familiar.

　　Residential buildings　Construction of residential buildings for overseas Chinese and expatriates stationed in China has also been a key area of the construction market which foreign contractors have penetrated. Indeed, the housing shortage in China has been very serious, especially in urban areas. The floor space per capita in urban area was only 4 m^2 in 1994, and it remained that almost 25% of families in urban areas had too few rooms (DoE,1995). Hence, people are very eager to improve their living conditions. Moreover some of their overseas relatives have given monetary support in home purchasing.

Foreign Participation in China's Construction

Up to now, most of the foreign participation in the construction industry in China has taken the form of consultancy services, ranging from engineering design to project management and supervision and training for the large Chinese construction companies that are usually stated-owned enterprises undertaking most of the major construction projects in China (Wills,1992).

Main Contractor

Traditionally, China has set up strict rules about the involvement of foreign general contractors in its construction industry. Foreign general contractors in China are only allowed to work on certain kinds of projects, such as foreign investment joint venture projects, World Bank projects, foreign aid projects and specialist trade projects where advanced technology is required and/or technology transfer to China is a feature of the project. If the local construction company is capable of providing the same end product, foreign contractors may then be prevented from taking part.

　　It is understandable why foreign contractors are limited to certain construction market in China. There are generally four reasons.

- China wishes to maximise and develop the use of its own labour and skills. For general building or civil engineering projects, local contractors have the experience and ability to undertake the job. There are some rules set up to protect the local contractors.
- Foreign contractors have higher operating costs which, in general, result in their prices or tenders being higher than those submitted by local companies. The tender price of the local companies will be much lower as the cost for labour and management of these local contractors will be lower too. Undoubtedly, local contractors are price competitors.
- A very long approval time will be needed if an overseas contractor is going to enter the Chinese construction market as an independent firm.
- Foreign companies are paid in Chinese currency for local projects, which is not a readily internationally convertible currency and has usually been undervalued.

Developers

Because foreign general contractors are rarely employed directly by the Chinese construction industry, direct investment is the other form of their participation in Chinese projects. They have invested in many property development projects, such as hotels, residential buildings and commercial projects.

Project Managers

Improvements in project planning, co-ordination and control are required in the Chinese contracting teams. They also need guidance on more complex and tall buildings since they are less experienced than foreign contractors in these aspects. In order to guarantee the quality and the efficiency of construction projects, foreign contractors have been employed as project managers to look after the projects, particularly joint venture projects.

Design Consultants

Design professionals are employed because their exposure to different types of engineering work and can offer new approaches to the design of the projects. For example, foreign consulting engineers were employed for the feasibility study for constructing a mass transit railway system in Shanghai Additionally, by working together, the consultants can pass their experience from the use of tools and equipment to design and organisation methods to their Chinese counterparts.

Specialist Contractors

Although foreign general contractors are generally restricted in China's construction industry, this discouragement does not apply to specialist contractors who are encouraged for technology transfer reasons. For example, foreign electrical and mechanical contractors are very active in the Chinese market. Since western technology is advancing so fast that, without adequate information and exposure to such advances, Chinese engineers may not have the capability to design complicated systems. Most joint venture projects, especially hotels and commercial buildings, employ foreign electrical and mechanical contractors.

Turnkey Contractors

Foreign contractors also participate in turnkey projects when the developers do not wish to be technically involved in any aspects of a project. The turnkey contractor will develop the project from inception to completion. Generally, the work let to Chinese construction teams is the construction of the structural frame, from foundation to superstructure. While the finishing and fitting work are undertaken by foreign contractors.

Problems Encountered by Foreign Construction Companies

The problems discussed in this section were raised by foreign contractors in several surveys including a 1985 survey and a 1987 survey of building companies, which had participated in Chinese construction industry, carried out by Institute of International Research in Hong Kong and a 1995 survey on Hong Kong construction companies, which had involved co-operation with Chinese construction companies. (Yen,1985;Chan,1995)

Construction Materials and Equipment

Shortage of Local Materials   One of the major problems concerning construction development in China is the shortage of construction materials. This problem has become more serious, especially in recent years, because of the rapid expansion of the construction industry in China. For example, even basic materials, such as timber, cement and steel, have to be imported to meet the demand. The shortage of local materials indicates that the increase in production of construction materials is much slower than the increase in construction projects. It is obvious that for imported materials, an additional transportation cost is incurred, so the construction cost will be increased.

Purchase of Foreign Materials In general, construction materials cannot be imported freely in China. The construction company that wants to import materials must apply to the Ministry of Foreign Economic Relation & Trade of China (MOFERT) for an import license. The MOFERT is very conservative in issuing import licences. Negotiation between the company and the MOFERT is usually required, and such procedures are very time-consuming and may take two or three months or even more to be completed. Delays in obtaining the import licence can often lead to delays in purchasing materials, and thus delay the overall construction schedule.

Transport of Materials Delays in work schedules may occur when construction materials are held up by transport logistics. Building materials are generally transported to the region by ship whenever possible. Otherwise materials are delivered by train freight transport. Delay of delivery frequently occurs even in major cities, such as Shanghai and Tianjin, because of lack of berths and trains. This problem is exaggerated by poor import-export planning and warehouse shortages. Ships may have to wait for a long period before cargo can be off-loaded.

Low Quality of Materials Nearly all finishing materials and engineering and mechanical systems have to be imported because of the low quality of local products. Hence, the construction costs are likely to increase and project schedule will possibly be affected by delays in delivery. In addition, the styles, design and colouring of local finishing materials are often conservative and limited in variety by Western standards. Furthermore, local high-quality products are very often exported to earn foreign currency. Therefore, usually only materials of secondary standard are retained for local use.

Bureaucracy and Insufficient Law and Regulation

Bureaucracy   The negotiation and approval period for doing business in China is usually long and feedback from the Chinese is slow due to the bureaucracy. Thus, the approval period for a business contract may be delayed for months. Indeed, local bureaucracy affects the whole construction process from its early stages, such as feasibility studies, to the later stages of construction or even after completion of construction works.

It is misleading to assume that bureaucracy is linked with corruption and can be solved in monetary terms. Traditionally, Chinese people prefer to do business with people who are well known to them and can be trusted. Thus, bureaucracy can be dealt with by creating better relationships and mutual understanding with the personnel involved. A good relationship between the top management of a contractor and important officials will be beneficial to that contractor in solving problems. Foreign contractors generally have to be prepared to run the risk and make allowances for potential delays caused by local bureaucracy when they negotiate or bid for a contract.

Insufficient Law and Regulation   Uncertainties in law-related aspects remain serious obstacles. Although China has made great efforts to enact appropriate laws since the economic reforms began, a number of fundamental and important laws still need to be enacted and enforced. Also there is a lack of a substantial official organisation in charge of the implementation of commercial laws. Because of the lack of a contract law and a complete legal system, contracts are workable in China only because the negotiation compensates for the incompleteness of the contract. Such practice is only suitable for simple contracts, however, and is not adequate for major international building projects in which foreign and Chinese developers, consultants, contractors and specialist contractors are involved. Due to the lack of a complete legal system and different contractual practices, a foreign contractor may be unable to apply the essence of a contract which specifies its obligations and rights in managing its subordinates in the mainland. Apart from the incomplete legal system which affects the enforcement of a contract, many internal regulations are confidential and are not disclosed to foreigners.

Local Labour Supply and Quality

Salary and Expenses   Cheap labour is one of the attractive elements which encourages foreign contractors carrying out construction projects in China. However, in spite of the cheap salaries compared with western countries, the total labour cost of a project is significantly higher than the salaries paid to workers. The reason is that companies with foreign investment have to make payments for retirement and pension funds, and unemployment insurance funds for their Chinese staff and workers according to the Labour Regulation published by the State Council of China. Moreover, housing or a housing subsidy fund has to be provided. Therefore, many foreign contractors in joint ventures have claimed that the total labour costs can amount to two or three times the individual worker's actual salary. Consequently, the under-estimation of such costs and expenses will lead to problems of budget overruns which may cause serious operating difficulties.

Unskilled Labour Although China has a huge labour force in the construction industry, it is largely unskilled. Skilled technical personnel accounts for only 4% of the total, that is around 0.6 million. Nearly 30% of the construction work force were originally farmers (Chan,1995). In general, Chinese workers carry out traditional builder's work, such as fabricating steel reinforcement, concreting and laying brickwork. They are not familiar with the work related to advanced techniques. Furthermore, material wastage is usually high because of poor organisation of work, poor workmanship and careless handling of construction materials. In addition, the site supervisor (usually) appointed by the Chinese party may not be familiar with the work to be supervised. Therefore, intensive training has to be provided for them before the construction work starts. All these, in turn, lead to an increase in construction cost.

Low Efficiency The efficiency of Chinese workers is usually lower than that of foreign workers because of the lack of incentives under the system where 'everybody eats from the same big pot', and where every worker is accustomed to receiving the same payment irrespective of performance. The shortfalls are compensated by employing more workers who are willing to work long hours. Towards the end of a project, shift work is often necessary to make up for the time lost caused by late deliveries or variations.

Management and Co-ordination Difficulties

Management Difficulties In many cases, Chinese personnel are involved in decision making at the management level of a joint venture. A foreign employee at the same level may earn ten times more than the Chinese counterparts. Chinese staff may thus bear grievances about the differences in reward. Such grievances may lead to low moral and negative attitudes towards co-operation with foreign personnel. Motivation can hardly be achieved by relying solely on the effort of the project manager staying in China. Close contact between Chinese and foreign staff at top management should be maintained, so that incentives can be created at the highest level.

Co-ordination Difficulties Co-ordinating construction teams from foreign countries and China is sometimes quite difficult because of the inadequate communication facilities in China. Communication between the site office in China and the head office in foreign countries is essential since arrangements for foreign materials purchasing have to be made in foreign countries. The service charge for international phone calls in China is amongst the most expensive in the world. Moreover, people coming from different parts of the mainland may speak different dialects and this also causes problems in achieving good co-ordination and communication.

Recommended Long Range Approaches to the Chinese Market

The foreign companies participating in the Chinese construction industry have been mainly from Hong Kong. This is not only because of the geographical proximity but also because of the better understanding of the cultural, traditions and current affairs in the mainland China. Many people in Hong Kong's construction industry can speak fluent Mandarin. They also know the importance of Guan Xi (Special Relation) for doing business in China and maintain many Guan Xi with the Chinese authorities themselves. (Chen,1994)

However, Western companies also have their own advantages for doing business with China, of which they may not even be aware. For example, the average scale of Western investment is larger and the level of technology introduced is generally higher. These facts are very much appreciated by the Chinese. Although the Chinese may prefer companies from Western Europe and America to those from Hong Kong and Japan for reasons of technology transfer and history, Western companies are usually not familiar with Chinese affairs. They do not know, psychologically, how the Chinese think and what the Chinese expect from the co-operation and, therefore, they often do not fully exploit their advantages. This has resulted in an extra-difficulty for them in approaching the Chinese market. The following recommendations are suggested to provide a guide for future Chinese-foreign co-operation.

- Up to now, the most popular way for foreign companies to do business with China is using the gateway function of Hong Kong (Chen,1993a). Western companies may use Hong Kong firms as conduits, or their Hong Kong offices as gateways into the Chinese market. Quite often the benefits to foreign companies of such an entry to the Chinese market may exceed the costs of dealing via Hong Kong intermediaries.
- Foreign companies can contact world organisations such as the World Bank, the International Monetary Fund, the United Nations, the Asian Development Bank, who provide funding for some major construction projects in China and call for international bidding for the services and equipment required.
- Overseas Chinese embassies and the representatives of major industrial departments of China are seeking to facilitate the Chinese-foreign co-operation. They usually provide a list of the projects requiring foreign participation and can also help foreign companies to make contact with Chinese partners. In addition, many overseas Chinese have set up their own consultancy companies to bridge the business gap between the West and China.
- Joint venture is the most popular way of doing business in China (Chen,1993a). It is impracticable for a foreign general contractor to work in China without the collaboration of a Chinese construction company because of the problems encountered in obtaining local labour and materials and in dealing with the many parties and government agencies involved. Hence in many cases foreign contractors provide project management, supervision and training when working with a Chinese construction company. It is crucial for them to maintain a good work relation and a mutual understanding with their Chinese partners in order to smooth out the problems which may occur. This also reduces business risk. It is worth mentioning that the personal connection with the Chinese government officials is one of the major reasons for the success of business. Foreigners usually have to co-operate with a Chinese company in order to obtain this benefit.

Conclusion

This chapter has pointed out that the major foreign participation in Chinese construction usually take the form of project management, supervision and training of local staff and consultancy services, usually in the fields of power generation, energy exploration, transportation, telecommunication and housing. Foreign general contractors are generally restricted from directly undertaking construction projects in China because China wishes to maximise and develop the use of its own labour and skills. Foreign contractors doing business in China usually encounter several problems including the shortage and low quality of locally produced materials, delays in delivery of production materials, bureaucracy and insufficient law and regulation, poor quality of local labour and management and co-ordination difficulties. To overcome these problems, several suggestions have been made including using Hong Kong connections with China, approaching major international organisations for their funded projects and approaching overseas Chinese organisations for their local contacts and information. Overall, joint ventures are regarded as the most fruitful organisational way to success.

8 Social Cost Benefit Analysis of China's Construction Investment

Since embarking on economic reforms and the open door policy in 1979, China has been achieving rapid economic growth and development. The Chinese government has made substantial investments in the construction sector, especially in establishing the Special Economic Zones (SEZs), bearing a close resemblance in many respects to export processing zones (EPZs) elsewhere in the world, as test-beds for development policies and suitable locations for foreign investors. Stimulated by the improvement in the investment environment and the preferential treatment provided by the Chinese government, a significant amount of foreign direct investment (FDI) has been attracted, which has been viewed as a major source of technology and an instrument of export promotion (Chen,1991).

From the viewpoint of China, most of the construction investments are regarded as public investment. It is, therefore, of interest to examine the extent to which the investment benefits society. To what extent does the contribution of the investment to national economic welfare, particularly in the SEZs, justify the expenditure? Or, could the resources have been better used elsewhere in the economy? This chapter analyses this type of investment by using a social cost-benefit technique. Since a large proportion of these investments was spent in the SEZs before 1990, this study will concentrate on the SEZs. Among the SEZs, the Shenzhen SEZ is the most extensive and economically mature one, it is thus taken as an example.

This chapter provides the framework of social cost-benefit first, followed by giving the general economic features of the Shenzhen SEZ, undertaking the estimation of the benefits and costs and the sensitivity tests and, finally, reaching the conclusion.

Economic Features of the Shenzhen SEZ

The Shenzhen SEZ covers a fenced area of 327.5 km² and shares a border with Hong Kong. The proximity to the Hong Kong market generates many obvious economic benefits for Shenzhen. The zone was set up, with substantial construction investment of over US$8 billion, on the site of a remote fishing village in 1979 (Chen,1991). The objectives of establishment of the zone included promoting exports, attracting foreign capital, creating employment opportunities, obtaining Western technologies and promoting regional development. Investment incentives were provided by the government, including exemption from corporate tax for a fixed term, customs duties on machinery imported for production and export duties, freedom to repatriate profits at a pre-specified rate and autonomy in many administrative aspects.

Since its establishment, the Shenzhen SEZ has become the fastest growing economy in the country with an average annual growth rate of gross domestic product (GDP) around 20% and industrial output around 50%. More than 70% of the companies operating in the zone involved joint-venture investment. The industries in the zone are export-oriented manufacturing with imported materials or materials from other parts of China. More than 80% of their products have been exported. The zone's exports contributed about 15% of the country's total exports by the end of 1993. The real estate development and service sector have received more than 50% of the total FDI in the zone and have contributed to most foreign-exchange earnings. (Chen,1994; EIU,1993; SSBC,1993)

The Framework of Social Cost-Benefit Analysis

Cost benefit analysis is a method of assessing the efficiency and profitability of the use of scarce resources in investment projects. Investment appraisal can be approached from a commercial viewpoint, in which case one generally speaks about private profitability of the investment, or it can be approached from the national point of view, where the term social cost benefit analysis is generally used.

Any investment project has to be assessed for its commercial viability by estimating its present value or internal rate of return. In the case of evaluating the net gains from a privately owned investment to the investor, this is done by estimating the present value of future net flows or private rate of return of the investment. When evaluating the net benefits of a public investment to the society, the rate of return refers to the social rate of return of the investment.

Net flows of an investment are estimated by discounting the future cash flows back to the present. By this process of discounting, expenditures and receipts (costs and benefits) which occur at different times in the life of the project are all revalued to make them comparable to present expenditures and receipts. They can then all be added up to give a single figure which is named the present value of the project. When the discounted expenditures of a project are deducted from the discounted receipts, the net present value of the project is obtained.

Internal rate of return is the rate of discount which makes the net present value of the project zero; i.e. the present value of the future flows of net benefits of the project equal its capital costs.

The decision rule for the present value criterion is: given the rate of discount, if the net present value of a project is positive, choose the project; if not, reject the project. From all possible projects, choose those projects with the highest net present value. The higher the positive present value of a project, the more beneficial it is to the investor.

The decision rule for the internal rate of return criterion is: if the internal rate of return of a project is greater than the interest rate, choose the project; if not, reject the project. From all possible projects, choose those projects with the highest internal rate of return. The higher the internal rate of return of a project, the more beneficial it is to the investor.

If factor and product markets were perfect and there were no externalities and indivisibilities, it is likely that private costs and benefits would coincide with social costs and benefits of a project. However, both product and factor markets in most economies suffer from a number of distortions due to factor immobilities, regulations, government interference through its trade, investment and pricing policies. In these cases, market prices do not reflect the true social opportunity costs of products and factors. The private rate of return on an investment may be greater or less than its social rate of return. This introduces the need for social cost benefit analysis.

The essence of social cost benefit analysis is to measure the net benefits from investment in a project to society rather than to private investors. In other words, social cost benefit analysis takes into account the true opportunity costs of resources to society. The resources used in a project and the output they generate should be valued at their true opportunity costs to society and not at ruling market prices. The basis for using opportunity costs, or so-called social accounting prices or shadow prices is that they correspond more closely to economic scarcity and strength of economic needs rather than market prices.

The approach used in this study derives originally from Little-Mirlees cost benefit technique (Little,1974) as modified by Warr (Warr,1986). The

Little-Mirlees method is well known. Warr used this method to evaluate the Bataan export processing zone in Philippines. In his study, the zone was treated as an enclave, a bounded area outside of the customs territory of the country. Emphasis was on the transfer of funds and resources between the zone and the rest of the country's economy. The aim was thus to study the net benefits and costs, as experienced by the rest of the country's economy, resulting from the existence of the zone, compared with the hypothetical case in which it was absent. Income distribution consideration within the country was disregarded in order to simplify the analysis. Changes in the income of foreigners received zero weighting and changes in the income of all national citizens were weighted equally.

Further modifications are required when this method is applied to China. Since the majority (more than 70%) of the firms operating in the zone were joint ventures (JVs), all the firms in the zone are treated as if they were JVs. Technologies transferred to the zone are all considered as labour-intensive.

Social Cost-Benefit Analysis of the Construction Investment

As shown in Table 8.1, the benefits of the zone to China include: foreign exchange earnings, employment opportunities, technology transfer, tax revenues and insurance premiums and Chinese partners' share of the net profits of JVs. The costs consist of: construction expenditure, administrative expenditure and electricity and water provided by the Chinese government. The estimation of each parameter will be discussed in detail.

This benefit brought in by FDI consists of the foreign currency that the zone firms convert into the Chinese currency to meet their domestic wage bill plus purchases of locally produced raw materials, less the value of their local sales of final products. The domestic wage paid by firms is included in the net employment gain. The products manufactured by the zone firms are mainly for export. Even if some of the products are sold in the domestic market, they are sold for foreign currency. Thus, only the purchases of domestic materials are taken into account in the estimation.

Conversion of foreign exchange into the Chinese currency Renminbi (RMB) is made at the official exchange rate. However, with exchange controls and domestic protection, the social value of foreign exchange in terms of the RMB received by China exceeds the value of the domestic currency the firms are given in exchange. The RMB is over-valued.

Table 8.1   Annual Components of Cost-Benefit Analysis of the Shenzhen SEZ (US$ million)

	1979	1980	1981	1982	1983	1984	1985	1986	1987	1988
Foreign exchange earnings	7.3	10.6	14.7	16.8	14.9	14.9	11.6	17.5	19.3	26.0
Employment	1.5	2.2	3.0	5.6	5.0	5.0	16.4	16.6	26.4	52.6
Technology transfer	0.1	0.1	0.1	0.3	0.2	0.2	1.7	2.8	4.8	7.2
Tax Revenues and insurance premiums	0.0	0.0	2.5	2.5	9.1	9.1	29.5	34.5	40.9	55.1
Net profit share of Chinese JV partners	-5.9	-4.9	3.5	-9.5	-3.6	-3.6	-19.7	-17.3	32.2	1.3
Construction expenditure	-16.9	-23.4	-27.0	-49.5	-51.6	-51.6	-140.9	-96.2	-67.4	-92.8
Administrative expenditure	-0.1	-0.1	-0.1	-0.3	-0.3	-0.3	-1.2	-1.1	-1.7	-4.1
Net benefit	-14.0	-15.5	-3.2	-34.1	-26.3	-26.3	-102.6	-43.2	54.5	45.3

Source :   The Shenzhen Statistical Bureau, the office for SEZs of the State Council of China and the State Statistical Bureau.

Therefore, the social value of the foreign exchange received from firms in the zone should be estimated at the shadow price. Estimation of the shadow price of foreign exchange for China has been made by the Shenzhen Foreign Exchange Adjustment Centre, and is referred to as the 'official adjusted exchange rate'.

The net gain of foreign exchange earnings is estimated as the local raw material purchases by the zone firms multiplied by the proportional difference between the shadow price of the foreign exchange and the official exchange rate. For example, in 1988, the shadow price of foreign exchange was 1.77 times as much as the official exchange rate, giving a proportional difference between the shadow price of the foreign exchange and the official exchange rate of 77%. This means that the net gain of foreign exchange earnings was 77% of US$34 million of the local raw material purchases. Thus, in this year, the net gain of foreign exchange earnings to China was US$26 million.

Employment

The Chinese government's interest in the employment generated by the zone obviously reflects the view that the social benefits derived from generating an additional job outweigh the costs. In economic terms, this may be interpreted as meaning that the wage received by the worker in the zone exceeds the opportunity cost of his or her employment elsewhere. The problems associated with measuring the opportunity cost of labour are well-known. In China, there are no minimum wage restrictions. Therefore, the market wage rate provides a good indication of the opportunity cost of labour, and the shadow wage is estimated as the market wage outside the zone.

The net gain from employment in the zone to China is thus estimated as the wage bill in the zone minus the estimated social opportunity cost of employing these workers. According to the State Statistical Bureau, the weighted average ratio of the shadow wage to the market wage in the zone is at 0.44. That is the opportunity cost of employment in the zone is 44% of the wage received in the zone. The net gain from employment is thus estimated as the actual wage bill multiplied by 0.56. This adjustment factor is applied to the wages paid by the zone each year.

Technology Transfer

The Chinese government hopes that Chinese firms would benefit from the technological knowledge of foreign firms entering the zone. However, most of them are involved in labour-intensive production and have little technological knowledge to offer which is not already widely available. Those firms which do have unique technological advantages (electronics firms are the best example) protect this knowledge carefully.

However, managerial techniques and methods of product quality control are inevitably transferred to the local middle level managers employed. When these managers move to employment elsewhere in China, the training they have received confers a benefit on the domestic economy, which is not captured in the wages they receive in the zone.

The net benefit to China from transferring of skills can be calculated in the following way. It is assumed that initially the zone firms employ foreign skilled personnel, whose shadow price is their wage (W) (assuming their consumption is entirely on imports and their savings are all repatriated abroad), and the local middle level managers the firms employ are paid a wage (C). As a result of training within the firms, the local managers become skilled and replace the foreign skilled personnel, reflecting the higher productivity due to the acquisition of skills. These local managers are referred as technical persons in this study.

The wage they could receive in employment elsewhere in China can be used as shadow wage which reflects the opportunity cost of this category of labour. This shadow wage is estimated as the wage received by the foreign skilled persons discussed above. Suppose that the real resource costs of training the local managers to the same level (in the zone the costs of training being assumed to be borne by the foreign firms) are K per year, then the net benefit of technology transfer each year can be calculated as: $(W-C+K)*N$, where N denotes number of technical personnel employed in the zone.

Tax Revenues and Insurance Premiums

The revenues raised from firms in the zone represent a clear source of economic benefit for the domestic economy. They consist mainly of taxes collected by the Chinese government and insurance premiums collected by the Chinese insurance companies. This is a net benefit to China because they would not be received if the firms were not operating in the zone. Firms which transfer to the zone from elsewhere in China, or foreign firms which would have entered China in any case, are exceptions which can be ignored

The tax rate is usually stipulated at 15% of profits. However, because of favourable treatment for foreign firms in the zone, the actual rate is estimated by the State Statistical Bureau at around 10%.

Net Profit Share of JV Partners

This net benefit to China is the JV's profit share minus the opportunity costs of the inputs provided by the Chinese partners.

The profit share of JVs to China is estimated by the total JV's equity owned by the Chinese partners multiplied by the private rate of return on the JV investment. When it is assumed the life of the zone to be 25 years, a 24% private rate of return is obtained (Chen,1993b).

As far as the opportunity costs of the inputs provided by the Chinese partners are concerned, most of the Chinese partners' contributions to the JVs relate to land, factory and residential buildings. The Chinese managerial contribution has been considered in the technology transfer from the zone to elsewhere in China. This is part of the government construction expenditure, which, if they were not spent in the zone, would be used elsewhere in the country. This benefit has been calculated by the author before (Chen,1993b).

Construction Expenditure

The Chinese government public expenditure required to set up the zone represents a clear economic cost. Some of this might have been required in the absence of the zone, for example on local roads. However, since the zone was constructed largely on reclaimed land, construction work would not have happened. The largest expenditure involved is specific to the zone. It includes construction of government-supplied land, construction of factory and residential buildings, provision of public utilities and communications and transportation facilities, levelling the site, seaport and airport construction, provision of international trade centres, research laboratories, hospitals and recreation grounds. The costs of government-supplied land, construction of factory and residential buildings have already been counted as inputs provided by the Chinese partners of JVs and thus are excluded here.

It should be noticed that only the construction investment in the zone consisted of both the Chinese government public expenditure and the capital invested by the foreign firms in the zone. Only the Chinese one is relevant to the social cost-benefit calculation and should be included.

Administrative Expenditure

The administrative costs of the zone have two main components: the opportunity costs of administrative personnel and of administrative buildings. The cost of the administrative buildings is included in the construction expenditure and thus is excluded here.

Electricity and Water Supply

The prevailing shortage of electricity in China and the relatively high expenditure involved in setting up the electricity network shows that the government provides subsidies for the electricity use. In practice, only part of commercial use of electricity is provided at the standard rate (subsidised rate) and the other part is charged at an adjusted rate, which is estimated by the State Statistical Bureau as the marginal social cost of generating electricity in China and can be used as the shadow price of electricity.

      Electricity supplied to the zone firms is charged at the adjusted rate. Since it would be charged at the same rate if supplied to other parts of China, it does not have a welfare effect on China and, thus, is irrelevant in the calculation of the net benefit from the zone. The same applies to water supply.

Discount Rate

China is faced with the shortages of foreign exchange and savings. The alternative to FDI is foreign loans. The international rates of interest on these loans are therefore usually regarded as the true opportunity cost of capital, which, being less distorted, are also supposed to reflect the marginal social productivity of capital. Real rates of interest on international borrowing are usually taken to be the appropriate real discount rates in this situation.

      These real interest rates rose over the period 1979-88 in a range of 5 to 9% in different kinds of hard foreign currencies. A weighted average of the real interest rate calculated by the Bank of China amounts to approximately 7.5% over the period.

Results of the Social Cost-Benefit Calculation

Figure 8.1 presents the net benefit from the zone in the period of 1979 to 1988. The calculation is based on a discount rate of 7.5% and an assumed life for the zone of 25 years, with a 56% wage difference between the firms in the zone and the firms outside the zone. The streams of annual net benefit estimated for the period 1979 to 1988 are assumed to remain at the 1988 value over the rest of the life of the zone. Therefore, a net present value of US$59 million and an internal rate of return of 10.7% are obtained. This is a high rate of return by the standards of public projects. It is clear from Table 8.1 that the benefits of employment, revenues raised and foreign exchange earnings are responsible for this outcome.

Figure 8.1   Net Benefit of the Shenzhen SEZ (1979-1988)

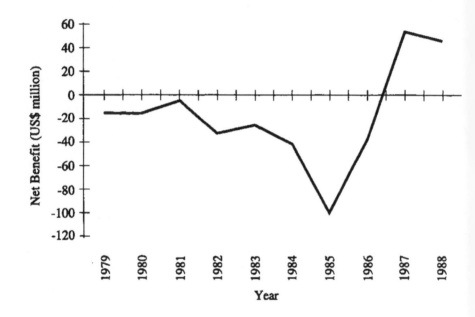

Omissions and Biases

Simplifying assumptions have been necessary for the evaluation. Some of them may have biased the estimated social profitability of the zone upwards rather than downwards. These include the following:

- The firms which enter the zone would not be present in China if the zone did not exist. In fact, a few non-Hong-Kong firms would presumably have invested elsewhere in China;
- An assumption of the majority of firms in the zone being JVs is also made, although about 25% of the total firms are either

Chinese firms or wholly-owned foreign subsidiaries;

- The JVs discussed covers all the sectors. The calculation of net profit share of Chinese partners is based on a 24% of JVs' rate of return. The Organisation for Economic Co-operation and Development (OECD)'s survey on 103 JVs in the zone suggests that the highest profit-making firms in the zone were hotel and real estate development, with an average rate of return on the investment of around 76% (Oborne,1986). The average rate of return on investment for the industrial firms in the zone was only 15% (Oborne,1986). The author's survey in 1989 also shows that real estate and construction companies earned more than a 50% rate of return (Chen,1991). This situation has not changed dramatically;

- The construction expenditure which the Chinese government incurred in the zone may be underestimated. Because the zone is located in Guangdong province, some of the Guangdong provincial government construction expenditure may have been spent in the zone, but this has not been taken into account in the analysis. This may reduce, although only slightly, the calculation of the infrastructure costs of the zone;

- The taxes received from firms in the zone are possibly overstated by the government for political purposes.

- The data of the costs for establishing the SEZ are possibly understated by the Chinese authorities because they are presumably anxious about demonstrating that the zone is a great success. Although the zone does seem to be a beneficial public investment, the social returns from it could be overestimated.

Sensitivity Tests

As far as the quality of data is concerned, most of the data used for the social cost-benefit calculations were provided by the Office for SEZs of the State Council of China and the Shenzhen Statistical Bureau, and, to the author's knowledge, are considered of relatively high quality and reliable (this is also confirmed by most of the firms interviewed in the zone during the author's survey). Data errors seem likely to be small. Even so, it is of interest to see how much the results of the social cost-benefit analysis would be affected by variability in the data by carrying out sensitivity tests.

Figure 8.2   Sensitivity Test: NPV - Variation of Discount Rate

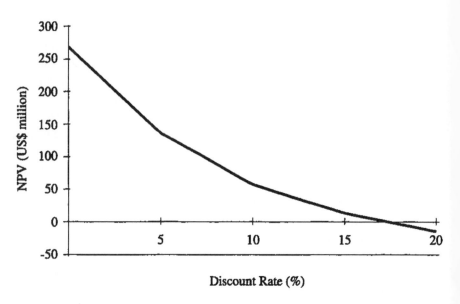

Discount Rate (%)

The discount rate is an important issue in the evaluation, since net benefits follow the familiar pattern of negative values from 1979 to 1986, followed by positive values in 1987 and 1988. Therefore, the net present values of the benefits are calculated for a wide range of discount rates from 2.5% to 12.5%. The results are shown in Figure 8.2.

The life of the zone is also an important variable, since the streams of annual net benefit estimated for the period 1979 to 1988 are assumed to remain at the 1988 value over the rest of the life of the zone. Therefore, the net present value and the internal rates of return are also re-calculated under three alternative assumptions about the life of the zone: a 20-year life; a 25-year life and a 30-year life. Figures 8.3 and Figure 8.4 present the results respectively.

The shadow wage of labour is estimated as the market wage outside the zone. This is because there are no minimum wage restrictions in China, which suggests that the market wage provides a good indication of the opportunity cost of labour. However, since the shadow wage used in the calculation is a weighted average one of different classes of workers and, moreover, since there are some kinds of government subsidies to workers besides their wages, such as housing and medical allowances, which may be

Figure 8.3   Sensitivity Test: NPV - Variation of Life of Zone

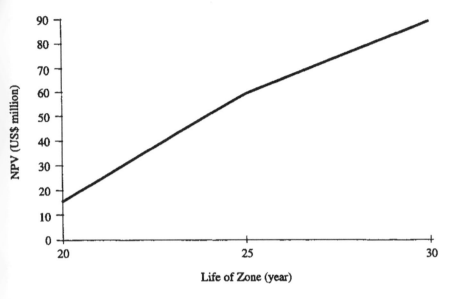

Figure 8.4 Sensitivity Test: IRR - Variation of Life of Zone

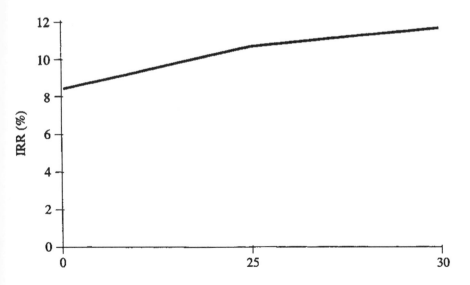

Figure 8.5 Sensitivity Test: NPV - Variation of Wage Difference

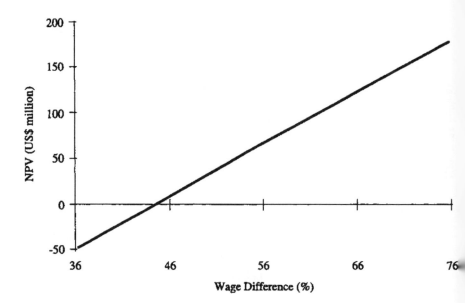

Figure 8.6 Sensitivity Test: IRR - Variation of Wage Difference

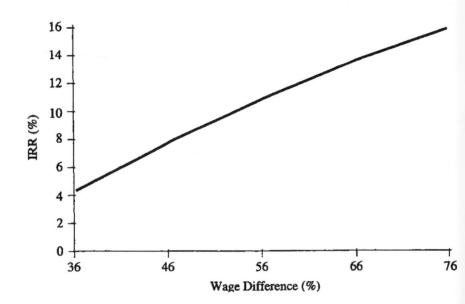

different between the zone and the outside zone, it is of interest to see how much the results of the social cost-benefit analysis would change if the assumed wage differential varies. Therefore, the net present value and the internal rate of return are re-computed for a wage difference among 36% to 76% (Figures 8.5 and Figure 8.6).

Another variation of the data is the construction expenditure spent on the zone. Besides the central government direct construction expenditure spent on the zone, since the zone is located in Guangdong province, some of the construction expenditure that the central government allocated to Guangdong province could be attributed to the zone. Since Guangdong province has experienced a rapid development of infrastructure construction, it would be unlikely that the proportion of the infrastructure expenditures which Guangdong province could attribute to the zone would not be spent elsewhere for infrastructure construction in the absence of the zone. Therefore, the diversion of the construction expenditure which could affect the calculation of the social costs of the zone seems likely, if at all, to be a small proportion of the total. Figures 8.7 and Figure 8.8 show the results of the re-computations of net present value and internal rate of return to see the extent the social cost-benefit analysis would be affected by the variation of the construction expenditure.

It can be concluded from the sensitivity tests, under most assumptions, the zone generates a positive net present value and an internal rate of return higher than the estimated real discount rate. This means that the social cost-benefit analysis can tolerate the assumed variations of the parameters.

Conclusion

This social cost-benefit analysis indicates that the Chinese government's construction investment, particularly in the case of the SEZs, is a beneficial public investment from the standpoint of China's economic welfare. Although considerable public expenditure has been incurred in establishing the areas, which were either isolated agricultural or fishery areas, the benefits, such as employment, foreign-exchange earnings, tax revenue and technical training, which the development has brought to China, have exceeded the costs. The infrastructure will remain and will benefit China in the long term. This is the major reason why the government has extended this type of development to the whole country.

Figure 8.7 Sensitivity Test: NPV - Variation of Construction Costs

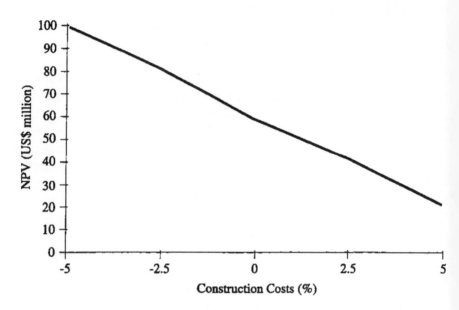

Figure 8.8 Sensitivity Test: IRR - Variation of Construction Costs

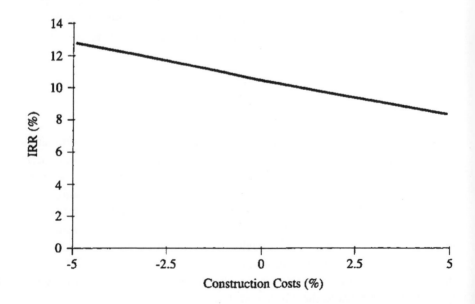

It should be noted that, since social cost-benefit analysis as a method of project appraisal has not been widely used in China, such a calculation has not been done as an a priori assessment for public investment. This study was the first of its kind. It does two important things: it provides a framework for analysis; and it attempts to quantify benefits. After more than fifteen years of operation, the SEZs have been considered an outstanding investment and have achieved many of the purposes for which they were instigated. The results of this study thus confirm to Chinese government expectations in general.

9 Pioneer Urban Housing Reform in China

Economic Background of the Urban Housing Reform

Housing in China has proved problematic for many years. Since economic reforms started to bite in the 1980s, urbanisation has become a token of modernisation and consequently, housing provision in urban areas has been a major social and economic issue. Virtually all the urban houses are the State's property and are public-owned. These are allocated to the urban population either by the work units or the housing bureaux in each city. The fundamental problems of China's urban housing provision have been: scarcity of supply, a low standard and under-maintenance. These problems have also affected the country's economy in that the land has not been valued correctly because of the neglect of site values in the allocation of land among competing urban uses and fixed housing arrangements in each city have reduced labour mobility in the economy. The government has borne the costs of housing construction and maintenance and made less financial resources available to economic development. However, it could be argued that it is housing scarcity which remains the Chinese government's most urgent problem to be solved.

China has made many efforts to build houses. It is estimated that housing production in Chinese cities has reached 200 million m² per year since the early 1980's (DoE,1995). However, the housing problem is still serious and it is believed that the major housing problem is in urban areas. Although there is a lack of detailed statistics on rural housing, there are apparently fewer major complaints from people living in rural areas about their housing. Families in rural areas usually provide their own housing including the finance. The economic reforms have meant that many rural families have more disposable capital and building costs in rural areas are lower.

For many years, scarcity of housing has been a major problem for urban people. In 1980 the floor space per capita was only 3.1m². By the end of 1994, this figure was around 4m². It remained that almost 25% of families had too few rooms. The usual form of urban dwelling is a flat. By Western standards, much housing in Chinese cities lacks basic facilities. In the early 1990s only 60% of flats had a kitchen. Further, the sizes of flats and rooms therein (often a small number of multi-functional rooms) are very small. It is anticipated that 150 cities and 2000 organic towns will be set up by the year of 2000 and 20% of the market towns will be modernised (DoE,1994). This is in addition to the about 30 million m² of old and unsafe housing in big cities, such as Shanghai, Beijing and Tianjin, which requires major maintenance work (DoE,1995). The demand is unlikely to be met by the prevailing Chinese resources and, thus, foreign investment is planned to be introduced within the next three to five years.

In urban areas, the major responsibility for providing housing rests with work units and housing bureaux. The work units include the State-owned enterprises (SOEs) and other public sector organisations who are responsible for providing housing for their employees. The housing bureaux are responsible for providing and allocating housing - mainly for the households who do not have work units to ask for housing or whose work units do not have housing stock to provide. These work units and housing bureaux provide more than 80% of urban housing in each local city council (Barlow,1988).

Traditionally, housing in China has been viewed as a non-useful cost of production that must be borne to produce the truly valued output which consists of manufactured goods. Effective housing reform involves not only finding a way to pass the responsibility for housing from public to private ownership but, more importantly, finding a way constructively to alter the traditional socialist treatment of housing. Figure 9.1 shows the housing reform plan set up by the central government since 1984. The major objective of housing reforms is to move gradually from a complete socialist-planned housing system towards a market-based housing system. The socialist-planned housing system is a rent mode which is marked by subsidised housing, low rent and works units and housing bureaux' responsibilities for providing housing which is, essentially, free of charge. Housing has been treated as an in-kind element of benefit for the employees. The market for housing has not existed and houses have not had a commercial value. A market-based housing system is, basically, a buy mode which is marked by private ownership and market rent of housing. Housing can be traded freely according to its market value. The reforms involve introducing market mechanisms in what has been an administratively managed urban housing system. The step is particularly dramatic in a socialist country where ownership of property has been considered anathema for decades.

Figure 9.1 A Market-Based Housing System

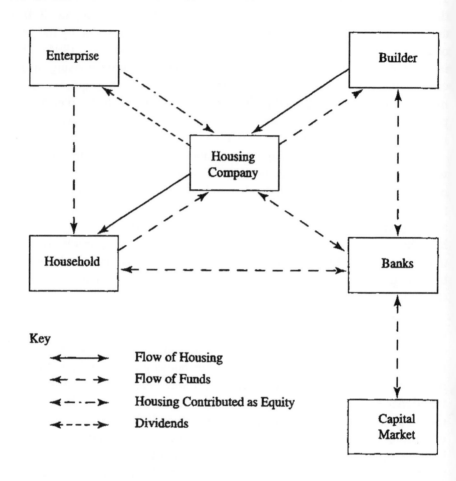

Source :   *'Urban Housing Reforms in China' , World Bank staff report,*
            World Bank, Washington D.C., 1995.

The initial housing reforms (1984-1993, called phase 1) focused on establishing a rental market for housing plus selling publicly-owned dwellings by providing large government subsidies. First, 14 cities were selected in 1984 as experimental centres for initial housing reforms. Second, to accelerate housing reform, in 1988, one of the most important initiatives of Chinese economic reforms was announced - the privatisation of housing. However, both the initial plans of 1984 and the privatisation initiative of

1988 have proved to be unsatisfactory, mainly due to the prevailing low rents, the lack of a housing finance system and the infancy of property law and regulations.

In 1993, the central government decided to modify the housing reform plan and put the housing system reform programme into effect in 1994 (called phase 2 reforms). The central issue in the design of the reforms has been how to privatise the housing stock, now in the hands of work units and housing bureaux. The first major step is to privatise and transfer the houses provided by the SOEs for their work force. The SOE work force, with a total number around 100 million, accounts for 70% of the work force in urban China and, along with their dependents, represents most of the urban population (The Economist,1995). The housing burden of the SOEs has been one of the fundamental reasons for their inefficiency and their incurred production losses. The World Bank has provided substantial assistance in promoting this move from the socialist-planned housing system to a market-based housing system.

At present, the phase 2 reforms have been still focused on establishing the rental market which was not realised in the phase 1 reforms. It is hoped that, gradually, rents will be increased to market prices. Therefore, the wages of the work force need to be increased as a prerequisite for paying the market rents. The first major measure is the setting up of Housing Management Companies (HMCs) in the experimental cities in order to free up the SOEs' obligation to provide housing for their employees. Then, the SOEs can use the money saved by not having to provide housing to increase the wages of their employees in order for them to be able to afford the market prices of housing.

This chapter analyses the phase 1 housing reforms and points out the reasons for the lack of success and the lessons drawn from them, and further studies the on-going phase 2 reforms including highlighting the problems.

Initial Housing Reforms Prior to 1994: Phase 1

The initial phase 1 housing reforms (1984-1993) focused on setting up a rental market for housing plus selling publicly-owned dwellings by providing large government subsidies. Furthermore, the reforms were seen as a way to ease inflationary problems. The hope was that saving for housing ownership would dampen consumption and divert demand away from consumer durables. The reforms were also seen as a means of raising funds to build new housing.

Reform Programme

The reforms were announced in 1984. Since then, housing has been regarded as a commodity and, therefore, should have a market value. Fourteen cities were selected to carry out housing reform in line with the central government policy. The local work units and housing bureaux increased the rent from 1% of monthly income for a standard family to 3% of their monthly income. The housing bureaux also set housing prices to encourage people to buy their own houses. However, since the housing market had not yet been established, market rents, the usual focus of analysis in considering the demand and supply of rental housing, had not been observed in China and the housing prices set by the housing bureaux might not reflect even the construction cost. There were neither carefully planned steps nor detailed regulations to implement the reforms. In order to encourage people to buy their houses and, therefore, to ease the burdens on SOEs for supplying housing and, at the same time, meet demand for new housing, both of which were growing rapidly in the 1980s, a large number of municipal governments adopted programmes in the mid-1980s to promote individual home ownership by providing subsidies, to the individuals who were willing to buy houses, of up to 70% of purchase prices (Wang,1989).

It soon became apparent that the 1984 programs were unable to generate significant housing sales. This is because, on one hand, the rents were still substantially low and, on the other hand, although subsidised prices had been provided, it appeared that people still could not afford to buy houses. There was no financial support system, such as a mortgage, available. In view of the worsening problems, in 1988, the central government decided to stop the subsidy promotion on housing sales and encouraged an experiment towards establishing a market-based system of housing provision. Privatisation of housing was announced, with the aim of introducing market mechanisms in what had so far been an administratively managed urban housing system. For a specific model, two small cities, Yantai and Bengbu, were selected in 1987 to experiment with substantial but restricted rent and wage increases. In addition, these two cities were encouraged to provide a financial support system to assist with house purchase. In 1992 the central government extended this initiative to make it applicable to all cities and set more gradual targets for rent and wage increases to substitute cash for in-kind payments.

The central government also encouraged the creation of 'housing funds', partly to support individual home ownership and, more generally, to augment the resources for housing construction. To manage the housing funds, local specialised institutions were established in Yantai and Bengbu as part of the 1988 reform experiment. Beginning in 1991, the newly created 'housing funds' had been supplemented with 'provident funds' funded equally by individuals and their employers and kept in employees accounts. Essentially, this amounted to creating a trust for earmarked funds with rates for both deposits and loans lower than other prevailing rates. However, in most cities, both the housing funds and the provident funds were handled by 'Real Estate Credit Departments', belonging to local branches of the People's Construction Bank of China or the Industrial and Commercial Bank of China. Most of the funds were deposited by SOEs as part of their welfare reserves.

Experience of Phase 1 Reforms

Progress of the phase 1 reforms has proved disappointing without any substantial solutions towards the housing problems. The government strategy of rent increase and promotion of home ownership has fallen short of its modest targets. Even the combination of low prices for housing and low interest rates has failed to generate significant housing sales to the general public, mainly due to low levels of income and savings and the disincentives to buy, created by low rents. The indication is that price adjustment, if not accompanied by other reforms, could end up making very little contribution to solving China's fundamental housing problems.

First, the rent increase did not result in the emergence of a truly effective rental market. This is because the increases in rents were not enough. The housing stock in the experimental cities appeared to remain as seriously mall-allocated as ever with doubled up families facing waits of up to half of a lifetime for apartments. The scarcity of housing has not been improved substantially.

Second, housing sales with large subsidies offered, although officially banned by the central government in 1988, were still common in many municipalities. This has occurred with the hope of reducing SOEs' burdens. However, this hope is a little unrealistic. While SOEs rid themselves of the necessity to provide the in-kind rent subsidy in the future, they may not recover even the construction cost of apartments sold in view of the reduced bids of buyers. Thus, the demand for housing was even increased.

Third, some aspects of the efforts to provide financial instruments for housing loan repayments remained rudimentary. For instance, low-interest rate loans could be provided to encourage purchase of housing, however, these could lead to inflationary pressures if the interest subsidies are no financed by explicit taxes on others. In contradiction, the short repaymen schedules, which were normally required with these types of loans, implied unrealistically high household saving rates which discouraged ownership Furthermore, the housing funds had not achieved their objective of promoting individual home ownership. Because the demand for individual loans was insignificant, most of the housing funds were used as short-term loans to SOEs for housing construction or purchase approved by the local government.

Fourth, much of the housing stock was seriously under-maintained which made old housing of low quality. Most housing still remains the responsibility of work units and housing bureaux. Meanwhile, few signs existed of preparing prospective owners to assume maintenance.

A critical shortcoming of the central government strategy up to 1993 was its inability to bring an end to the work units and the housing bureaux direct obligations for employee housing. Given that current rents would have had to be increased 10 to 30 times in real terms to reach commercially viable levels, it was doubtful whether such a target could realistically be achieved, in even gradual steps, and remain acceptable to consumers. As is apparent from the lack of progress achieved so far, consumers were always likely to resist even gradual rent increases if these were not fully compensated by income growth. This is because raising the proportion of income spent on rent, as envisaged in the central government strategy, represents real income reduction. The affordability analysis that underlied the approaches in the phase 1 reforms was fundamentally flawed as it ignored expenditure incurred by SOEs for providing their employees' housing and, thus, was unavailable for compensating wage adjustments when rents were restructured. In effect, the strategy was geared less towards establishing a market-based housing system than to mobilising more resources for housing. There followed a growing discussion among the central government and SOE managers aimed at identifying an effective and feasible alternative strategy. There was a need for bolder reforms.

The picture that emerged was of a permanently distorted rental market in which the benefits of market allocation were lacking with losses on housing sales extending into the indefinite future and with chronic tension between the rationed markets (State-allocated housing) and unrationed markets (commercial housing).

The Housing System Reforms since 1994: Phase 2

Since 1994, drawing lessons from the failure of the phase I reforms, the central government has announced further housing system reforms. These are associated with the whole country's economic reforms and economic progress.

Having succeeded in facilitating fast economic growth through the introduction of new management arrangements and market mechanisms, the central government has begun fundamental reforms in fiscal, financial, macroeconomic management, enterprise and labour systems in order to move towards the next stage of economic development. Central to these reforms is SOE reform, as the problems of SOEs lie at the root of many difficulties in other areas. To improve SOE management, the current strategy to develop a 'socialist market economy', officially adopted in 1992, calls for more aggressive measures to increase accountability and efficiency of the SOE sector as a whole.

As noted earlier, the SOE work force and their dependents represent most of the urban population (The Economist,1995). It has become apparent that housing is one of the major burdens of most SOEs and many of them have claimed that having to provide housing has led to loss of profits or loss of production. Consequently, it is widely recognised that establishing sustainable housing and social security systems is a crucial prerequisite to broad economic restructuring.

New Reform Programme

The new housing reform programme announced in 1994 by the central government includes:

- raising rents by a big margin: from 0.13 to 1.00yuan/m^2, about 10% of monthly income of a standard family, (compared with 3% of monthly income during phase 1 reforms) and, in 2000, to 3.25yuan/m^2 (17% of monthly income) at current prices. The employees of the SOEs would be fully compensated by wage adjustments and gain more freedom of choice.
- selling publicly-owned dwellings in the cities to their tenants at three kinds of prices: standard price for high-income families, low-profit price for middle-income families and preferential price for low-income families. The preferential price is 350yuan/m^2 which means that, for a standard family, a flat of average floor space will cost three times its annual income.

- offering mortgage loans over 25 years.
- allowing buyers to sell their houses in the real estate market after 5 years of ownership.

This program aims to commercialise housing by establishing a market-based housing system. The central issue is how to implement the program, what measures and in which order they should be taken. The central government set up a Leading Housing Reform Office under the State Council in charge of the implementation of the housing reforms. With consultancy aid from the World Bank, a new approach is being developed to pioneer this new programme which will focus on converting the in-kind housing benefits into cash wages and setting rents and sale prices at levels which cover at least the full cost.

A Market-based Housing System

There is general agreement of the desirability for a market-based housing system where end users select housing solutions from a wide range of options offered by independent commercial providers. In such a system, SOEs would not have any direct responsibility for their employees' housing other than providing full, competitive wages. Figure 9.2 shows the current housing system in typical Chinese cities.

Supply and financing of housing, functions now performed mainly by employers in China, would instead be carried out by independent housing consumers, suppliers and financial intermediaries in the market system. In order for commercial suppliers to sell or rent housing without subsidies, sales prices would have to recover all costs over the economic life of the housing. Consumers would deal directly with suppliers to choose housing according to their needs and affordability. As costs of housing assets are large compared to the homeowner's income or to rental receipts, long-term credit is an essential ingredient of a well-functioning housing market. In order to ensure and sustain the housing market, financial institutions will have to offer competitive returns on deposits and charge interest rates that cover the cost of funds and their administration. Credit risks need to be controlled by strengthening the legal framework that provides for effective property and mortgage rights. Further, a fully developed housing finance system should include a variety of institutional channels and financial arrangements to allow secondary mortgage markets to emerge and encourage the participation of different types of investors.

Figure 9.2 Current Housing System in China

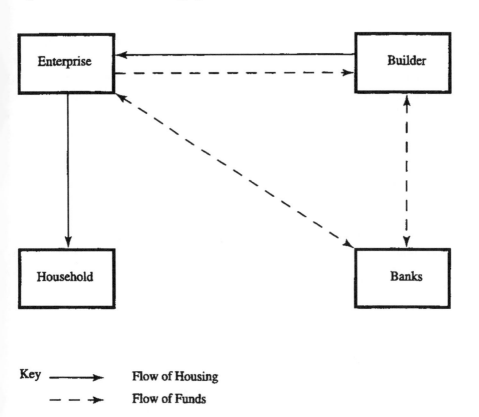

Key ⟶   Flow of Housing

– – ➤   Flow of Funds

Source :   *'Urban Housing Reforms in China' , World Bank staff report,*
                 World Bank, Washington D.C., 1995.

Implementing Measures

The phase 2 reform started with substantial increases in rent which would be fully compensated by wage increases. As this measure redirects the flow of resources that are available already and used in the system, the rent and wage adjustments would be affordable. An effective alternative strategy, however, would need to have devices to deal with key issues of transition, including the initial absence of the market-based system of housing, finance, wage adjustment formulae and affordability problems faced by specific individuals and unprofitable SOEs. This led to the establishment of the 'Housing Management Companies'.

Housing Management Companies (HMCs) As an alternative strategy to initiate a market-based housing system and to help the divestiture of state-owned enterprise housing, joint-stock housing management companies (HMCs) have been established in some cities such as Beijing, Yantai and Ningbo. Their task would be to make housing a fully functioning contributor to the national economy, largely by correcting the major deficiencies of the supply of housing stock. The HMCs would administer the housing stock contributed by the SOEs as equity capital in return for ownership shares. Clearly defined ownership rights and corporate governance structure would help reinforce these characteristics.

At the beginning, all housing would be owned by HMCs which would rent out apartments at market determined rent levels paid for by wage increases made possible by the complete elimination of need for the SOEs to bear any housing expenses. From this starting point, the HMCs would be ready to sell apartments, as well as continue to rent them out. Gradually, more and more apartments would be sold as people became more familiar with what ownership means and as younger families made life financial plans including housing saving during their earning years.

Over time, some occupants would choose to sell their accommodation to others and become renters if they liked, which would be allowed as part of a policy of freedom of choice. The resources presently devoted by the SOEs and housing bureaux to upkeep might be transferred to the new owners in the form of wage increases. Since there appears to have been chronic under-maintenance, the individuals, as owners, might undertake more maintenance than is covered by the wage adjustment, which would be anti-inflationary in taking expenditure away from other things. Transferring ownership to occupants would be a small price to pay for relieving the SOEs and housing bureaux of the burden of supplying housing and for achieving the long run goal of efficient housing arrangements.

Initially, HMC customers would primarily consist of the employees of SOEs' that, originally, owned the stock because it is likely that not only the SOEs, which would be the share holders, would want to give priority to their own employees but also commercial rents and prices would not be affordable to employees of other entities whose wages had not been adjusted. There are other types of companies, such as profitable private and joint-venture companies, which usually have cash capital but no housing stock because both the central and local planning authorities restrict them to build new residential houses for their employees. It is hoped that successful access to the housing market would induce these companies to invest in HMCs by making cash equity contributions. It would also be necessary to encourage more HMCs and other housing suppliers to enter the housing market and compete in order to prevent a few HMCs from monopolising the market.

Wages Compensating for higher costs of renting or buying housing, the SOEs would provide cash wage supplements to allow workers to pay higher rents or mortgage payments. The supplements would be financed from savings on housing expenditures that are no longer necessary. Since the housing stocks of SOEs were contributed by the SOEs, as their equity shares to the HMCs, the dividend profits on these shares would help to increase the wage supplements for the SOEs' work force. The supplement should be determined on the basis of typical housing occupied by workers holding comparable jobs, not the specific housing unit occupied by a particular individual; and it would be made a part of the comprehensive wage and subject to adjustment as a whole, not according to changes in housing consumption in the future.

Finance Commercial levels of housing rents and increased cash wages of individuals would make commercially priced housing loans for HMCs and individuals feasible. Financial projections have been prepared for all HMCs established by the end of 1993, reflecting current operational plans. A World Bank study shows that HMCs will be able to generate considerable cash flow and dividends even if they increase the standards of operation and maintenance to much higher levels than current ones (World Bank,1995). The World Bank sensitivity analysis also shows that the levels of interest rate and capital investments have the most significant effect on the financial viability of an HMC; and the debt-service ratio (ratio between cash flow from operation and debt service) tends to be very sensitive to such key parameters.

Problems Associated with the Phase 2 Reforms

This section addresses several major problems associated with the new approach and highlights the need for further work.

Non-Equity SOEs and Non-Equity Work Units According to the plan for establishing HMCs as a solution to the housing problems, equity SOEs can contribute their housing stock to the HMCS. However, for those SOEs and work units who do not have housing stock as a contribution to join HMCS, they have the problem of increasing their employee's wages to meet the increasing rent or to buying their accommodation. There are two typical types of family in China as far as housing is concerned. One is that there is at least one member of the family belonging to an equity SOE which has housing stock to contribute to the HMC or, at least, one who works with a profitable joint venture or a private company which can pay a comparatively high salary compared with local standards. This kind of family appears to be able to afford the increasing rents. However, the other type of family is where nobody in the family works with an equity enterprise which has housing stock or all members of the family are unemployed. Therefore, this kind of family would be unable to afford the rent increase. In this case, what would the government do? Should the central or local government provide subsidies for their living, then the burden would be added to the social security system? This would contradict one of the major objectives of the enterprise reform. However, should the central or local government not make any effort on this matter, consequent social problems would arise. Therefore, measures will need to be considered to help this type of family.

Possibility of Monopoly Because only a limited number of HMCs are being established, and these are supported by the central government, they may begin to monopolise the housing market. They would take advantage of the reform and manipulate the housing market. This would, in fact, create more market distortions and possible consequent corruption. Monopoly and corruption would also be likely to happen in the housing finance market because only a limited number of banks are authorised by the central government to deal with housing finance. There is no effective securities market in China. The banks who have the right to deal with housing finance could easily monopolise the housing finance market and, therefore, create more corruption. Policies and regulations to prevent monopoly and to establish more companies to function as HMCs, more financial institutions and a security market to deal with housing finance should, therefore, be considered by the central government.

Lack of Knowledge of Housing Economics and Expertise There has been little attention paid to the need for better knowledge of housing economics and management that would make it possible to devise more effective selling terms to estimate how much housing can be sold and to help housing reforms contribute to the economy of China. Reforms devised in the absence of this knowledge, run the danger of tinkering counter- productively, and unleashing unanticipated effects. There is a severe shortage of skilled housing personnel in China to understand and implement the reforms. Therefore, professional training is needed urgently.

Weakness of Regulatory Framework   The proposed new housing reform programme requires strengthening a number of legal and regulatory instruments in China, including those governing registration and valuation of property, property rights, landlord-tenant relationships, foreclosure, eviction, condominiums and financial regulations. At present, contracts are used to overcome specific deficiencies in the national legal framework. However, further development of the regulatory framework will become increasingly important as the housing market develops.

Conclusion

The establishment of a market-based housing system to privatise housing is the ultimate objective of China's housing reforms. Increasing rents has been the major step adopted so far since the housing reforms started in 1984. There is relatively little experience with the sort of system envisaged under the reforms, where houses have been sold below cost with many, if not most, families continuing to live as tenants paying below-market rents. Therefore, it is not surprising that the housing reforms so far, whilst having moved away from a complete socialist housing system, have gone only a small part of the way to a market-based housing system.

The phase 1 reforms have proved disappointing. On the economics side, failure to follow cost-based guides in setting rents and housing sales prices contributed to the lack of success. Rents are set below costs and the link between the value that people place on housing and the cost to the country's economy has failed to be appreciated. On the management side, the critical shortcoming of the strategy is its inability to bring an end to the enterprises' direct obligations for employee housing.

At present, the phase 2 reforms are focused on the setting up of a rental market. However, the strategy should establish commercial levels of rents, higher cash wages and long-term mortgage financing that will lead to viability of ownership options. Therefore, provisions must be made to allow households, who wish to buy units and can accumulate the necessary downpayment, to obtain mortgage loans. The success of HMCs would create a viable rental market which would attract further investment from private sources and insurance funds. However, as home ownership spreads, it would present a more important area of private investment. Because new housing would, increasingly, reflect consumers' tastes and budget constraints, the intrusive regulations and guidelines governing housing unit size and other related aspects would lose much of their justification and would need to be replaced with a set of ordinances to safeguard health, safety and environmental considerations. It is hoped that, with rents and housing prices allowed to find market levels and with housing divorced from the SOEs and other public sector organisations, the fundamental gains from the housing reforms will be realised fully.

Several major problems associated with the phase 2 reforms have been identified. More attention should be paid, and effective measures be adopted, towards the problems, especially on the legal side. Otherwise, the reforms could end up making very little contribution to solving China's housing problems, with the danger of worsening the situation.

10 Sustainable Development: A Sino-British Comparison

Although the United Nations Conference on Environment and Development (UNCED 1992) is viewed as the watershed in securing an international recognition that environmental concerns must transcend political and national boundaries it should be remembered that the Rio Summit was itself only one stage in an international dialogue which began with the Stockholm Earth Summit (UN Conference on the Human Environment in 1972) and which was further progressed at the World Commission on Environment and Development in 1987.

It may well be argued that the significance of Rio stems not from its articulation of a global environmental ethic, so much as a recognition that, in the 20 years since environment had first been perceived as an international issue, it was no longer relevant to consider national economies in isolation, rather it was appropriate to refer to a global economy and the extent to which economic growth was both influenced by and in turn itself influences environmental quality. It was also the case that, over the same period, significant changes in political ideology in a number of parts of the world saw the move, by a number of previously centrally planned economies, to the development of a market led economic approach, a shift which further underpinned the concept of a global economy.

These two factors, a recognition of a global economy and an increase in the number of nation states pursuing market economic approaches, highlighted the inadequacy of analyses identifying environmental concerns and environmental management as issues relevant to the developed but only of marginal interest to the developing world. The interdependency evident between national economies, whether developed or developing, which had prompted the notion of a global economy was equally valid in the context of the identification of the global environment.

This chapter considers the relationships between sustainable development, land use planning and environmental planning and their value as a policy tool. It explores the significance of China as a very large developing economy and its actual and potential environmental impacts at a national and international level, justifies the validity of evaluating China's Agenda 21 at this stage in its development and discusses China's Agenda 21 and the opportunities and challenges which it poses in terms of its operationalisation. It also provides an outline of the United Kingdom's experience to date in its formulation and implementation of Agenda 21 and explores it as a possible framework for application in the context of a developing economy like China.

Sustainable Development: Policy Tool or a Visionary Concept?

The arguments surrounding the development of and the concepts which underpin sustainable development have already been extensively reviewed elsewhere (Pearce,1993; Redclift,1993; Palmer,1994). In the context of this chapter, however, it is important to establish from the outset that the concepts of *sustainable development, land use planning and environmental planning/management,* although frequently used interchangeably in the academic and professional literature and in practice, are by no means synonymous. This is particularly important in the arguments to be presented here since the concern is to look at the ways in which the vision of sustainability can be realised or operationalised via the practice of land use planning and environmental planning. These latter, although both clearly having a theoretical basis, are in essence active processes with concrete outcomes which are capable of being evaluated in both a qualitative and quantitative sense.

In a succinct analysis of the conflicts surrounding these concepts, Blowers (Blowers,1992) states that:

> Sustainable development is a vague concept that, at once, offers a comprehensive, consensual and conservative approach able to weld together disparate and conflicting interests in the environment and development. But because it is vague and its implications poorly understood, in practice it offers few clear solutions. Anyone can sign up for sustainable development so long as it requires no specific commitment to do anything which will threaten their material interests.

He then goes on to identify what he sees as the essential features of *environmental planning* as an overarching approach to environmental management and, in so doing, distinguishes it from land use planning. He argues that:

Environmental planning brings together two distinct elements. By *environmental* we mean all the physical, (natural and manufactured) resources that support human activities. By *planning* we intend to convey a political system that is able to create and co-ordinate policies over different time periods and spatial scales; that can identify targets and methods for implementing them; and that is capable of monitoring and evaluating outcomes. Environmental planning is, therefore, not the same as land use (spatial or town and country) planning, although land use controls may well be part of the process. Environmental planning is a comprehensive approach to environmental management which has three basic features: it takes account of future uncertainty by a *precautionary approach*; it reflects the *integrated nature* of environmental processes and policies and it takes a *strategic approach* to decision making.'

Rydin (Rydin,1993) also emphasises the distinction which exists between land use planning and environmental planning. In her consideration of the impact of British planning she states that there is a growing role for land use planning in achieving environmental policy goals. She argues that:

As a mechanism for integrating a variety of environmental concerns with location-specific land use decisions green planning has much to offer. There are a number of mechanisms by which this can be achieved, environmental impact assessment (EIA), waste disposal plans, pollution control concerns within development control. Development control has also been used to deal with perceived inadequacies in environmental policy such as protection of ground water, post closure pollution control for waste disposal sites and protection of the aquatic environment.

In addition to identifying the policy instruments and measures which bring together the roles of the land use planner and the environmental planner she observes that:

the process of integrating environmental and land use planning is not a matter of applying technical environmental data to existing planning decisions. It involves a whole new array of consultations and interactions in decision making. It brings new interests into the mediation process that planning engages into.

Whilst this is without doubt a truism it leaves implicit the issue of whether land use planners, environmental planners and local communities share the same view of what constitutes the environment which the planning process seeks to protect.

Lucas and Chambers (Lucas,1996) argue that:

> there is a need for policy makers to recognise that environment is not conceptually discrete and that it has a complexity of meaning and that this must be translated into policy action. By failing to recognise that there is no common understanding of environment within society and that notions of environment have historical, theoretical, cultural and perceptual contexts, they argue that policies geared towards environmental protection or strategies which seek to incorporate environmental standards may be misplaced unless developed following extensive consultations.

It is important that those responsible for both the formulation and implementation of environmental policy take note that environment is a socially constructed concept and has a range of meanings. When a land use planner talks about environmental conservation he/she may well be defining what constitutes the environment to be conserved and what constitutes conservation in terms with which a member of the local community or a potential developer may have little or no rapport.

Whilst acknowledging the richness of the theoretical issues surrounding the sustainability debate and the role of planning within it, we are more concerned with those concrete proposals and policies which are being advanced in the name of sustainability. This may leave an uncomfortable gap between policy and action/theory and explanation but that is an issue to which we will need to return at a future date.

It is against this complex theoretical and empirical background that the chapter seeks to draw out the opportunities and tensions which emerge from an analysis of the environmental strategies which have been introduced by the Chinese and United Kingdom governments in response to UNCED's call for the international community to address the concept of and to secure, via Agenda 21, a strategy for sustainable global development. It appears therefore that whilst land use planning is a well developed policy tool, particularly in the United Kingdom, and an emerging one in China, the concept of environmental planning and environmental management are at an earlier stage in their development and currently lack coherence. We concur, however, with Rydin that 'green' planning has much to offer and the analysis which follows is based on the view that environmental planning is an increasingly important feature of contemporary land use planning strategies and that there needs to be a greater linkage between the two. In the context of China versus the UK experience the opportunity exists for cross fertilisation of ideas, an issue to which we return in our conclusions.

The significance of the analysis which follows is that it clearly identifies the contrasts between Agenda 21 in the UK, as a strategy which is largely responding to issues associated with an advanced capitalist society undergoing restructuring in response to global recession, and the emerging and rapidly expanding Chinese economy. In making this comparison, however, it is acknowledged that environmental and resource degradation are not exclusively the consequence of high levels of economic development. It is, of course, the case that inadequate economic development can be equally environmentally damaging.

Taking the latter first, from the perspective of a 'limited development economy' for example, rural poverty and population pressure often combine to exert stress on natural systems (a tendency to overgraze pasture land), erosion of productive agricultural land as a result of inappropriate farming techniques, depletion of productive forestry as a consequence of its use for fuel coupled with deforestation associated with attempts to expand arable agriculture. Similarly in the urban context unplanned population growth, associated with rural/urban migration, which is inadequately supported in infrastructural terms inevitably results in, *inter alia*, increased atmospheric and water pollution which in turn results in higher incidence of environmentally triggered diseases.

By comparison the picture to emerge from a rapidly expanding economy can be shown to be equally environmentally damaging as, for example, agricultural land gives way to urban sprawl with its associated transport and other infrastructural demands and industrial and commercial expansion places increased demands on energy usage etc.. This is not to argue, however, that there is a simple choice to be made between development and the environment, rather it is the case that there needs to be a mechanism whereby measures are adopted to restore, sustain and protect natural systems and maintain environmental quality during the early stages of the development process (WB,1992a). With these comparisons between developed and developing in mind, what makes an analysis of China's environmental strategy so interesting is the fact that the geography of the country, coupled with differential rates of economic growth in different provinces and cities, means that we can simultaneously observe conditions which characterise both a limited development economy and a rapidly expanding economy within one national context. It is against these contrasting rates of development that China is seeking to introduce its Agenda 21.

Whilst without doubt, the conditions referred to above present a significant challenge, it is also the case that the current stage of development of the Chinese economy provides an opportunity to incorporate environmental provisions into the national development strategy from a relatively early stage, rather than the 'retrofit strategies' which characterise for example, the European Union in general and the United Kingdom in particular. In short it is possible, despite its considerable environmental difficulties, for China to make a significant contribution to global sustainability.

What is being sought therefore is a model or policy framework which assists in informing the debate around and the development of policy in the context of sustainability. In his paper, Roberts (Roberts,1996) points to the value of adopting an ecological modernisation approach:

> Ecological modernisation suggests that it is possible to integrate the goals of economic development and environmental protection and that through this reconciliation synergy's will be generated which can be harnessed and put to good use. Whilst this concept (ecological modernisation) appears at first to offer a pain free route way to the achievement of sustainable development, in reality choices and compromises still occur and require resolution.

Hajer (Hajer,1996) identifies three different interpretations of ecological modernisation:

- as institutional learning - in which industrial and administrative organisations learn from critiques of conventional industrial society put forward by the environmental movement, and from this develop modes of economic development which are compatible with the environment - this interpretation assumes that existing institutions can internalise ecological concerns;
- as a technocratic project - in which radical environmentalists argue that the ecological crisis requires more than social learning by existing organisations and that ecological modernisation as institutional learning offers a false solution to very real problems - this interpretation argues that without fundamental structural changes in the economy, environmental problems are left unaddressed;
- as cultural politics - this reading of ecological modernisation sees the debate on environmental problems as a reflection of wider debates on the preferred social order, this interpretation emphasises the nature and processes of social and political debate about what sort of society - and environment - we want and how to negotiate social choice in order to arrive at the preferred option.

From these three interpretations it is possible to identify three distinct and distinctive modes of response. Each of these responses represents a stage towards what Simonis (Simonis,1989) refers to as 'the necessary and feasible harmony between man and nature, society and environment'.

The critique advanced in Hajer's second interpretation - ecological modernisation as a technocratic project - points to the inherent weakness of end-of-pipe solutions, or the assumption that new technologies can be relied upon to counter new environmental damage. This implies that positive action, based on the precautionary principle and the desirability of ensuring that prevention rather than cure is the guiding principle of practice, should be emphasised. Whilst the merits of this second interpretation are self-evident, they do not, in themselves, provide a basis for progressive change in most western societies. Rather, it is the first and third of Hajer's interpretations that represent the most fertile soil in which to cultivate a new mode of regional and urban planning.

The first interpretation - ecological modernisation as institutional learning - is the most commonly adopted mode of reorientation. At the core of this interpretation is the need to break with the past, to move away from a reactive mode of response to environmental problems and towards a mode of operation that avoids the need for reaction through the adoption of anticipation. This implies, in Hajer's, that environmental degradation should not simply be viewed as an external problem, instead environmental concerns should be integrated within policy-making. The use of procedures such as EIA can help to ensure that such integration occurs.

However, despite the substantial progress which has been made in the manufacturing sector in some countries towards the achievement of ecological modernisation in accord with the conditions of the first interpretation, further progress inevitably means moving towards the conditions specified by Hajer in his third interpretation - ecological modernisation as cultural politics. The third mode suggests that there are choices to be made as to 'what sort of nature and society we want' (Hajer,1996). In defining and determining these choices the role of discourse is a central. Thorough discourse future scenarios can be constructed and, having demonstrated the implications of such scenarios, alternative goals and pathways can be identified. This mode of interpretation and operation is similar in some respects to a 'strategic vision mode of analysis and planning (Roberts,1990)'.

As this chapter unfolds the multifaceted interpretations which Roberts draws out from Hajer's work are seen to be those same factors which now impinge on China's developing environmental strategies. It will become evident that institutional learning has and is taking place, that the technocratic stance, although necessary in the context of aspects of China's environmental programme is recognised as limited in application and that there is a recognition that environment and economic prosperity are not mutually exclusive but that competing tensions can only be resolved via extensive discourse.

China's Global Importance in the Development of Sustainability

What is it that links China's economy and environmental policies such that they emerge as important factors in securing global sustainability?

Our stance is that the importance of China's Agenda 21 derives from (a) the economic and potential environmental impact of its economic development in global terms, and (b) the fact that its extensive and ongoing economic, political and social transformations, are underpinned by a national development strategy which is geared to 'sustainability'. The validity of this assertion is reinforced by the growth of the Chinese economy, as highlighted by a comparison of its GDP in 1970 (US$93,244 million) with that for 1993 (US$425,611 million). Industrial growth for the same period increased from 38 to 48 per cent and in manufacturing from 30% to 38%. Within these aggregated figures it is important to note that the average annual industrial growth rate over the period 1980 to 1993 has been 11.5% compared with 8.9% in the decade between 1970 and 1980. The annual growth rate in manufacturing has been more even, averaging 11.1% over the period 1980 to 1993 compared with 10.8% in the preceding decade. It is also important that, although for ease of argument, we present national data, within these are considerable regional variations which make the formulation and implementation of national policies extremely problematic.

The picture which emerges from the above is an economy characterised by considerable growth in the industrial and manufacturing sectors. This scale of growth, however, brings in its wake a need to address environmental impacts, not merely from a national perspective but, given the scale of activity, in international terms as well. It is of course possible that, in pursuing the imperative of economic growth, this may wholly or partially obscure the debate surrounding environmental considerations. Indeed this view is reinforced by the Economist Intelligence Unit (EIU,1995) who argue that:

China has been slow to recognise the gravity of environmental degradation which has resulted from 17 years of growth. Where policy is willing, implementation will be selective, so that critical new investment is not discouraged nor fragile domestic industry burdened. Economic priorities in certain sectors and localities will prevail over environmental considerations, notably in China's interior where development is urgent and political fall-out containable. China is unlikely to commit more than a minimum expenditure on clean technology except where this brings obvious, observable efficiencies and economies, as in energy, natural resource exploitation, water conservation, forestry and agriculture. China will target environmental legislation and approvals at foreign-funded ventures and established domestic corporations. Agency funding will be sought for improved standards in population centres.

Given the foregoing, coupled with the consequential global impact of failing to secure genuine environmental improvements in China, the potential for its Agenda 21 to secure sustainable development should be evaluated at this early stage of its development so as to highlight potential weaknesses and to close gaps by observing good practice elsewhere and incorporating it, in an appropriate way, into the Chinese environmental programme.

China and the Global Environment

Before embarking on an evaluation of China's environmental strategy it is important to first establish why the success of the latter's Agenda 21 is of vital concern to the international community since, only then, can we proceed to a second issue, namely a meaningful discussion of the mechanisms by which the vision set out in China's Agenda 21 can be achieved, in a manner which will complement rather than impede economic development and growth.

Considering the former prompts the question, what are the characteristics of China's geography, economy and social structure which are the significant factors in the debate concerning sustainability and on which its Agenda 21 are predicated?

Ryan and Flavin (Ryan,1995) are of the opinion that China is putting the concept of sustainable development to a severe test and on an unprecedented scale. They cite the following as the principal challenges to building and delivering a sustainable development strategy: population pressure; consumption of natural resources; economic growth; consumption trends; and agricultural production. These factors are considered briefly in turn.

Population Pressure Population pressure is a key factor which underscores the need for the introduction of an effective sustainability strategy. This is perhaps more readily appreciated given China's population growth from 574.82 million to an estimated 1185.17 million over the period 1952 to 1993. China's recorded population in 1993 amounted to some 1,178 million (approximately 22% of global population) a total which is projected to grow to 1,255 million by the year 2000 and to peak at 1500 to 1600 million between 2020 and 2025, if strict population controls are enforced (CSNA,1989). It is also the case that during the period from 1970 to 1993 the urban population grew from 17 to 29 per cent. Both these parameters are indicative of the extent to which policies which are inevitably geared to provide for this rate of population growth and directed, inter alia, to agricultural provision, energy production and consumption, housing provision, manufacturing industry and transport infrastructure will consistently challenge environmental quality.

For example to sustain this level of population growth it is estimated that raw coal production will progressively reach 1.4 billion tons per annum and the annual level of electricity generation will rise to a total of 1.3 billion mwh. In addition, and in recognition of an expansion in manufacturing industry, it is expected that an integrated transport infrastructure will be created to facilitate the transport of 2.1 billion tons per annum of goods by rail and with a seaport handling capacity of 1.1 billion tons per annum. The potential environmental impact of these policies is self evident.

Consumption of Natural Resources In environmental terms an exponential growth in the consumption of natural resources presents a significant challenge. The per capita level of natural resources is low with land, forest cover and water resources at 36 per cent, 13 per cent and 25 per cent respectively when compared to world per capita levels (Wang,1989).

In addition to these rather daunting statistics there are also problems associated with energy and mineral resource deficiencies. China's reserves of coal are less that half the world average in terms of immediately exploitable coal reserves on a per capital basis. Oil and gas are even less abundant and, while there is hydroelectric potential, it is generally inconveniently located with respect to centres of population. Moreover, the country's fuel conversion efficiency is low (28 per cent) when compared with rates of 40 to 55 per cent in North America and 60 per cent in Japan (Lees,1991).

Economic Growth This has already been outlined above but it is worthy of re-emphasis that China's economy is in transition and characterised by dramatic economic growth over the period since DENG Xiaoping's market reforms. As stated previously comparative data for GDP shows that it has expanded from US$93,244 million in 1970 to US$425,611 million in 1993. Table 1.1 in Chapter 1 more clearly identifies the expansion of the Chinese economy over the period 1988 to 1995 with projections to 1996.

Consumption Trends Whilst it is not intended to consider this aspect in detail here it is relevant that the weighted annual growth rate for private consumption in China for the period 1980 to 1993 averaged 7.9%. Its significance is evident when compared with the weighted averages for the same period for low income countries at 2.2% and for high income economies of 3.0% (WB,1995). It is argued that personal consumption trends are a useful barometer of actual and ongoing environmental impacts.

Agricultural Production It concerns, here, the tensions which exist between the need to secure higher returns vis-‡-vis agricultural activity versus the pressure to achieve urbanisation. It is argued that China can support 950 million people at a good standard of living based on the country's land resources but it is also the case that 72% of China's population live in rural areas and that the percentage of national income which comes from agriculture is only 25.4% (SSBC,1995). Per capita farmland is about 0.08 hectares whilst cropland accounts for only 10% of China's land area with both the per capita and total quantity of arable land decreasing. Chen (Chen,1991) estimated that arable land has been reduced by approximately 366,000 hectares over the preceding decade. The progressive loss of agricultural land is perhaps partially explained by Ryan and Flavin's assertion that the World Bank data suggests that land on the outskirts of cities that is rezoned as industrial immediately soars to 15-20 times its agricultural value. Succinctly stated agricultural land must be made to give the greatest return.

A measure of the environmental impact which accompanies this recognition is evident from its Agenda 21. This acknowledges that, by the close of the present decade, China will have increased food and cotton production and will have achieved a grain yield of 500 million tons per annum, a level of agricultural activity linked to a projected level of chemical fertiliser production of 120 million tons per annum.

From this brief overview what can we realistically identify as the principal environmental problems which face China as a consequence of the complex interaction of its geography and the stage it has reached in its economic development?

China experiences a range of environmental problems which, at present, appear to be worsening. As stated previously differential economic growth provides for significant spatial variations in environmental quality On the one hand, problems commonly found in an underdeveloped agricultural society such as soil erosion, deforestation and desertification are becoming increasingly evident whilst on the other, industrial growth and urbanisation has and continues to lead to severe chronic pollution.

A clear picture emerges from a consideration of certain key industries and utilities. Industrial expansion has placed increasing demands on an electricity industry which is largely reliant on coal fired installations. Indeed coal accounts for roughly 73% of China's commercial energy consumption. This has, however, progressively reduced from a high of 92.3% in 1957. Its level of coal consumption significantly contributes to China being the world's third largest contributor to global carbon dioxide emissions which account for approximately 9.4% of the world's annual carbon load from the burning of fossil fuels. It is also the case that the economic significance of coal is much greater than in other countries who have extensive coal reserves such as India. In India coal accounts for 57% of commercial energy consumption compared to China's 73% (UN,1994). The environmental impact of industrial energy production and consumption should not be left, however, without a reference to rural China, where air pollution is a particular problem resulting from the combustion of crops, dung, and wood for domestic heating and cooking. Energy in the form of biomass supplies about 80 per cent of demand for heating and cooking in rural areas (Florig,1993). With these patterns of fossil fuel consumption there is a tendency toward higher levels of indoor rather than outdoor pollution and with higher levels in the rural as opposed to urban areas. This is not to imply that ambient external levels of pollution are acceptable since this is far from the case but rather to emphasise that death from respiratory illnesses is almost three times more likely in China's rural areas than in its cities (MPH,1988).

In the context of water resources, water quality issues continue to be the single most serious pollution problem resulting from small-scale industries. A 1989 nation-wide survey clearly illustrated that many provinces had high levels of pollution in rural areas caused by small-scale industries. It is the case that the percentage of individual waste water undergoing treatment has risen dramatically from 13% in 1981 to 81.7% in 1993.

In the populated rural areas then, environmental problems are more marked, particularly in the eastern rural areas where small-scale industries proliferate. Over the past 15 years, the rural collectives have emerged as the most dynamic element in the Chinese economy, but their pollution of their local environment, particularly in terms of contamination of drinking and crop irrigation supplies, is considerable. A comparison between the environmental impact of rural collective firms and all industrial enterprises found that the ratio of waste water discharges to output of food processing, textiles and pulp and paper industries are higher for the rural collectives firms than for all industrial enterprises in three of five cities studied (WB,1992b).

The ongoing potential for rural industrial pollution to increase is evident from an analysis of the rural enterprises' total output value which registered an annual average growth rate of 25.3% between 1985 and 1990 and the fact that they now employ about one-quarter of the rural workforce (Dwyer,1994). The limiting factor in remedying this form of environmental degradation is that the rural enterprises often use outdated equipment and cannot afford to invest in pollution abatement technologies. It is also the case that in the rural areas poverty and poor educational standards among the peasant population contribute directly to China's environmental problems. Half of China's counties still do not have rural extension services which, when combined with high illiteracy rates, means that it is difficult to disseminate ecologically sound techniques.

A more universal problem which impacts on China's progress towards environmentally sound practices is the apparent complexity of its environmental land management administration. The environmental management system in China is administered at three levels. The top tier is represented by the State Environmental Protection Commission, the second tier comprises the provincial environmental bureaux, whilst the lowest and third tier is formed by local city or rural district environmental bureaux. For a large development project it is significant that approval is required from each of the environmental bureau, planning bureau and land administration bureau at least at the provincial level. It is the case, however, that co-ordination is less than systematic and conflicts are not uncommon. The absence of a decision-making forum which incorporates individuals from the environmental, planning and land administration arms of government, at the appropriate level, to co-ordinate project assessment and ongoing management is seen as a significant limiting factor. This is a consideration to which we return at a later stage.

Environmental Remediation in China: The Economic Impact

It is perhaps relevant to briefly consider the costs associated with environmental remediation/clean up. Environmental degradation is extensive, particularly with respect to the pollution of waterways both inland and coastal with costs likely to be significant. Table 10.1 provides three estimates of potential expenditure expressed as a low, medium and high prediction.

The low cost estimate is based on the government's planned investment in environmental protection in 1991-95. It reflects only the minimum investment necessary for environmental protection and excludes research and development expenditure necessary for the identification and refinement of environmental protection technology and relevant education and training. In the case of pollution control this level of expenditure merely targets 9,000 enterprises.

Since the Chinese government estimates that it would cost RMB 200 million to retrofit all its ageing factories with appropriate pollution control equipment the planned investment would have to be doubled to secure the improvements sought. In light of this it is reasonable to extrapolate values so as to reflect the medium and high estimates by inflating the low range estimate by 25% and 50% respectively. The level of investment to secure significant environmental recovery would demand expenditure equivalent to 1.86% of GDP and 2.23% of GDP respectively. At present investment amounts to 0.4% of GDP (SEPC,1994). It is also the case that the environmental equipment industry in China is underdeveloped so that significant foreign exchange will have to be secured to provide the necessary software and hardware. It is clear that this latent demand for environmental control equipment could form the basis for an emerging 'green' industry. Given the scale of costs involved and the enormity, both actual and potential, of the environmental damage which could ensue, a systematic analysis of costs and expected benefits is a prerequisite to the allocation of scarce financial resources. It is evident that successful economic development is underpinned by the rational use of environmental resources and on minimising, as far as possible, the adverse impacts of development projects. This can only be achieved by improving project selection, planning design and implementation.

Whilst it is the case that much of the cost of environmental cleanup and ongoing protection will demand government funding, China's public sector expenditure gap presents a significant barrier. Decentralisation of tax collection to local government, coupled with a profit making culture at this level of government, a political preference for investing in employment rather than ecology, and the social costs of rising levels of unemployment are all likely to severely weaken the ability of government, at both central and local level, to finance ecological reforms.

Table 10.1 Estimated Cost of Environmental Recovery and Protection in China

	Low Range		Medium Range		High Range	
	Cost (b. RMB per yr)	% of GDP	Cost (b. RMB per yr)	% of GDP	Cost (b. RMB per yr)	% of GDP
Cost of pollution treatment and protection	23.00	0.85	28.75	1.06	34.50	1.28
Air pollution	8.00		10.00			
Water pollution	9.00		11.25		13.50	
Solid waste and noise protection	6.00		7.50		9.00	
Cost of ecosystem recovery and protection	17.15	0.63	21.44	0.79	25.73	0.95
Forest	0.75		0.94		1.13	
Grassland	4.50		5.63		6.75	
Soil erosion	4.00		5.00		6.00	
Desertification	0.80		1.00		1.20	
Flooding and water control	7.00		8.75		10.50	
Biodiversity	0.10		0.13		0.15	
Grand Total	40.15	1.48	50.19	1.86	60.23	2.23

Source : *[SEPC, 1994].*

In addition to the economic position above it is also the case that improvement in China's environment will require internal political stability coupled with international support. There is no lack of awareness of the difficulty which faces China. The government has become increasingly aware that environmental and natural resource depletion is counter productive to long term development. In consequence politicians are clearly more receptive to the implementation of measures which ensure that development projects take both the environment and natural resources into account.

It is not intended to discuss China's Agenda 21 here, this is considered in more detail in Section 10.4. Here key aspects of current strategic responses are briefly outlined to point to areas of future activity or policy gaps. Having identified areas for future consideration as part of China's Agenda 21 strategy, recommendations are put forward in the conclusion section.

China: Responses and Policy Gaps

Whilst progress is being made there is considerable need for more co-ordinated efforts. In policy terms environmental protection is still a relatively new item on China's political agenda, emerging as it did as an issue just after the end of the Cultural Revolution in the late 1970s. Whilst it is the case that heavy industry, manufacturing and infrastructural projects have necessitated environmental impact statements as part of their development from the early 1980s, such statements have been somewhat cosmetic. Whilst environmental protection legislation stipulates that environmental assessments are to be carried out for construction projects there is no similar requirement for smaller scale developments. It is also the case that the process is not readily open to external scrutiny.

Environmental degradation of the countryside increased during the early 1980s as many of the rural reforms encouraged practices which were not sustainable. Despite environmental protection legislation being introduced in 1989, China has yet to fully implement a programme of environmental policies. Where attempts are being made the momentum appears to be slowed by attempts on the part of central government to achieve consensus between interested parties. In addition uneven distribution of natural resources and population, referred to earlier, further complicates attempts to formulate policies at the national level.

There are concrete examples of how an integrated policy approach has had demonstrably beneficial effects. During 1980-1988 energy consumption was reduced by approximately 37%, in part due to the shift in industrial structure (Sinton,1994). While relatively higher energy prices undoubtedly had some effects on energy conservation those reforms only marginally raised raw material prices. Energy efficiency during the 1980s was achieved as one element of Chinese-style economic reform whereby investments in improving the technological capabilities of state-owned enterprises bridged the 'technology gap' thereby enabling the central state to administer and implement environmental regulation (Polenske,1993).

Despite the appearance, during the 1980s, of market mechanisms, political pressure from local government remains the main driving force in encouraging investment in environmental control since raw materials, i.e. water, timber and coal, remain artificially underpriced. Market mechanisms have, however, helped to control some aspects of environmental degradation, in particular pollution in the state-owned industries. It is the case that if there is steady economic growth and no major shifts in policy the next decade will herald improvements in the urban environment.

To deal with problems associated with rural industry, however, will necessitate considerable government investment coupled with regulation and effective policing. Given the earlier comments on the need to improve agricultural output whilst avoiding environmental problems associated with intensive farming techniques to maximise arable yield part of the solution lies in making agriculture more attractive. This will require higher prices for agricultural products and a degree of land consolidation to maximise farm efficiency. Given the relatively slow return on this in economic terms it may be that government will be reluctant to prioritise this as a policy initiative. Over and above technological improvements, management efficiency has a major contribution to make in environmental control. Zhao states that industrial pollution in China could be reduced by 30% simply by improving technology management in enterprises (Zhao,1990). Pollution abatement equipment is frequently incorrectly installed and lacks maintenance.

At a general level education may well be useful in reducing certain forms of environmental degradation such as noise pollution and littering. Within factories, staff training on various aspects of pollution control began in the early 1980s. The number of people being trained in environmental studies grew throughout the 1980s and is likely to continue to grow. It is reasonable to assume that the raising of general levels of education will have far reaching consequences. It may well also be the case that in the absence of an evident environmental stance which is based on practice rather than promise, China could face resistance to the purchase of its goods and products in the face of an international move towards creating a more level playing field vis-‡-vis manufacture in which ecological damage or dumping is increasingly viewed as anti-competitive.

Environmental Action: Prospects and Policy Initiatives

It is clear that its development trajectory presents it with a significant challenge in achieving what has been identified (in the context of the member states of the European Union) as a key environmental policy objective namely promoting sustainable growth while simultaneously respecting the environment. It is acknowledged that China clearly recognises the importance of their sustainable development strategy for the rest of the world. Indeed the National Environmental Protection Agency in outlining the formulation of the Chinese national plan for sustainability stated that:

> China is a developing country with about 1.2 billion people. Therefore, the issue of environmental protection and sustainable development is a component part of the global issue of environment and development. The success or failure of China's environmental protection will have an important bearing on the environmental protection of the world and the realisation of the goals for sustainable development of the world. However, as a developing country with a big population and a low level of development in technology and economy, it is facing the dual tasks of developing its economy and protecting its environment. (OECD, 1995)

The inherent tension which this statement highlights is more explicitly stated in China Agenda 21 as follows;

> For a developing country like China, the precondition for sustainable development is development only when the economic growth rate reaches and is sustained at a certain level, can poverty be eradicated, people's livelihoods improved and the necessary forces and conditions for supporting sustainable development be provided.

Clearly this emphasises the need to implement a development strategy which simultaneously facilitates China achieving a level of economic activity which creates and supports these necessary conditions but which incorporates effective environmental checks and balances. In acknowledging that China seeks to secure development it is, however, pertinent and not merely semantic to point to the distinction between development and 'out and out growth'.

Whilst, however, it is acknowledged that appropriate environmental strategies must be developed to meet national, cultural and governmental priorities, rather than the imposition of an international prescription, it may be informative to take a retrospective view of UK developments in this area together with a prospective view of emerging Chinese strategies, as the two countries seek to implement their respective Agenda 21 programmes.

In doing this the authors acknowledge that much of the experience emerging concerning the operationalisation of Agenda 21 derives from developed countries where policies are being applied in retrospect i.e. the retrofitting of industry or the modification of existing policies and strategies. In making such a comparison, therefore, we accept that we are not comparing like with like in contrasting current UK practice and emerging Chinese approaches to sustainable development. It is argued, however, that this should not detract from the value of presenting approaches which have been adopted within the UK thereby enabling a more detailed analysis than is possible here, over a longer time scale and by those familiar with and intimately involved in formulating policies in China which seek to achieve the aims and objectives of China Agenda 21.

The UK Experience: Sustainability in a Developed Economy

Having established the context of China's Agenda 21 and its policies to date it is appropriate to turn to an overview of Agenda 21 development in the United Kingdom, with particular reference to the mechanisms and systems which have emerged to secure its aims and objectives. This section is, therefore, concerned with the implementation of Agenda 21 from the perspective of an advanced economy and one in which there is a long tradition of land use planning, development control and an associated hierarchical governmental mechanism for planning enforcement.

In pointing to the UK as a possible model, however, we recognise that its model is one of central domination and that in the planning context this is not without its problems. A model which relies on national, i.e. centrally derived strategies has the potential to negate the validity of the region as the appropriate spatial unit to secure sustainable development. Although not discussed here the German and Dutch models may well repay a careful examination.

Without fully exploring the United Kingdom governmental and planning system it is appropriate to provide an overview. For those who need to have a deeper and more detailed appreciation, Rydin, HMSO and DoE all provide a useful account (Rydin,1993;HMSO,1995; DoE,1992a).

To appreciate the relationship between land use planning in the United Kingdom and the development of an environmental strategy it is important to understand the relevant tiers of government via which planning policy is both formulated and implemented, together with their respective powers and duties. It is also the case that it is only by considering the historic traditions and current attitudes to the environment and its use that one can begin to understand how the UK Agenda 21 has developed and, in so doing, highlight where we can learn from past experience and at the same time perhaps identify key issues which could inform evolving frameworks within developing economies.

Governmental Administration in the United Kingdom

The basic governmental structure in the UK is best described as operating at three levels, these are respectively the district (local), county (regional) and the national level. By way of complication, in Urban Metropolitan areas, and since 1995 in some more rural areas, the functions of the local and regional tiers have been combined so as to create a number of Unitary Authorities. In the context of land use and environmental policy, which are our primary considerations in this paper, District and Unitary Authorities have powers to make decisions relating to planning and linked policy issues relevant to their administrative area but, in making these decisions, they must reflect on and act in accordance with both and national policies. Subsumed within their range of functions is a responsibility for Agenda 21 in terms of both policy and practice. Monitoring and evaluation, is undertaken at both the local and national tiers. (DoE,1996)

At the national level UK central government is administratively complex and comprises a number of Departments and Ministries which are responsible for the development of policy. Together these form the permanent executive which informs the legislative function of government. Clearly it is Parliament which is responsible for the enactment of legislation which relates to Agenda 21 and environmental issues subject only to its obligations to the European Parliament.

Here, it more concerns with the administrative functions of government. The UK government has, as stated above, a complex administrative system comprising a series of separate but, as will become evident, overlapping responsibilities. Each ministry or department is divided into a series of directorates or divisions. The department with the most significant influence on Agenda 21 is the Department of the Environment (DoE). This was formed in 1970 to assume the responsibilities of the former Ministries of Housing, Local Government and Public Buildings and Works. The responsibility of the DoE reflects its constituent parts and includes, inter alia, planning, local government, housing, new towns, construction, inner city policy, environmental protection, water, countryside affairs and government property and land holdings. In addition there is also a Water Directorate which has responsibilities for setting standards for and maintaining environmental water quality. Likewise, there is a Directorate which deals explicitly with air quality, climate and atmospheric conditions and toxic substance control and a separate division with responsibility for pollution control and wastes. Finally there is a division which has a remit for environmental policy at both a national and international level. (DoE,1990)

As can be seen from the above, the remit of these directorates overlap such that planning policy, pollution and environmental protection issues fall within the scope of a number of divisions. To further complicate matters a number of other governmental departments influence Agenda 21 issues and policies including the Department of Health, the Department of Employment and the Ministry of Agriculture Fisheries and Food. This latter have responsibility for rural protection, control of some conservation policies and marine protection.

The complexity of and cross departmental responsibilities within central government inevitably impacts on the development of Agenda 21 to the extent that, of necessity, Agenda 21 needs to incorporate and take account of existing policies and practices and, as a consequence, has a tendency to be rather more reactive than proactive in some critical areas. It is this aspect to which, in part, we referred earlier in saying that the UK's Agenda 21 can be described as 'retrofit' since its evolution is constantly needing to be accommodated within a well established and entrenched, both governmentally and professionally, administrative system.

At local level, local government similarly divides responsibility for environmental protection and Agenda 21 issues between both its two local administrative tiers but also internally within individual municipal administrations. This has clear implications for the practical application of Agenda 21 policies. Local administrations have a more limited geographical responsibility and, being an elected body, they clearly represent a spectrum of political views. This in turn, not uncommonly, leads to individual authorities, albeit geographically adjacent, being potentially somewhat removed in terms of policy priorities and practices. Such differences in ideology can give rise to conflicts between authorities over issues such as, for example, transport, industrial land use, economic development and regeneration. Such differences as may arise are clearly superimposed on those which may be evident from a difference between the local, regional and central tiers of government. A lack of consistency between local government authorities in different parts of the UK has likewise led to some confusion regarding Agenda 21 policy and practice.

Although acknowledging a degree of inconsistency between authorities it is the case that there has been a genuine attempt to involve local communities in the Local Agenda 21 process by incorporating community views into the development plan process. This is particularly evident given the government's commitment to increasing people's awareness of the part that their personal choices can play in delivering sustainable development, and to enlist their support and commitment in the coming years (HMSO,1994;French,1995).

UK Agenda 21 - Policies and Practice

Within this administrative hierarchy the UK Agenda 21 adopts a strategic environmental assessment approach which necessitates relevant issues to be considered at all levels from national to local, at the same time as recognising the international dimension (LASG,1994). The focus of the UK's approach is the application of a series of key principles based on action at the local level via a requirement for local authorities to implement a *Local Agenda 21* initiative within their administrative area.

In essence the UK set out six key action areas for its Agenda 21. These are all seen as operating at a local level and comprise:

- managing and improving an individual local authority's own environmental performance;
- integrating Agenda 21 aims into an individual local authority's plans and policies;
- awareness raising and education;
- consulting and involving the public;
- partnerships;
- measuring, monitoring and reporting on progress towards sustainability (DoE,1996).

It is a specific responsibility of local authorities to directly undertake action to achieve items one and two above and to become actively involved on a broader community basis with the later four areas.

Whilst these principles are of interest as part of the wider environmental debate, items one and two can be clearly identified with a local authority's planning responsibilities vis-‡-vis sustainable development. The integration of sustainable development aims within local authority's policies and activities has tended to focus on several key areas which are intimately linked to land use. The land use planning system has therefore, become one mechanism for promoting sustainable development through strategic and local planning policies which encourage, inter alia, energy efficient patterns of development, reducing the need to travel and protection of landscape and habitats. One manifestation of local government's proactive stance is evidenced in such initiatives as the 'Environment City' exemplified in Leicester.

It should not be assumed, however, that because Agenda 21 has been and continues to be incorporated into the planning process that it is universally accepted nor that its underlying philosophy is without its critics.

Conservation and environmental groups have indeed been very critical of the UK Agenda 21 Action Plan (FoE,1994;CPRE,1995). Whilst the UK has been clear to set out its agenda and to adopt environmental targets, these are seen to reflect the British traditions of resource conservation and have been criticised in terms of their generality.

Despite these criticisms, in the aggregate, it would appear that as a policy tool UK local government has employed and is employing Agenda 21 at local level to bring together and strengthen existing commitments towards the environment, local economic and social factors and to local democratic representation. Whilst approaches vary between authorities most operate by local steering groups and utilise existing council systems (LASG,1994).

Local government is thus central to Agenda 21 and hence the development of sustainable development policies. In this context and as a general guide to local authority policy development (LASG,1994) summarises five ways in which local authorities in the UK have been influential in actualising Agenda 21 in practice, these are:

- as major consumers of resources;
- as a force for change in the market place;
- as a model for other organisations;
- as providers of information and know how;
- as providers of enabling services;

- as networks;
- as consensus builders and lobbyists.

Agenda 21 in delivery is therefore via a local authority integrating its activities across the spectrum of its regulatory and enabling functions. It is by such an approach that local variations in environmental conditions and constraints are accommodated. Conversely this could, however, without clear national guidelines and monitoring lead to wide variation in the effectiveness of Local Agenda 21 policies between areas. Consistency has, however, been achieved via a variety of organisations and mechanisms. Many of these have been fostered by and build on existing planning and environmental frameworks. Some specific mechanisms have been introduced in direct response to the Rio Summit. The more important of these include the development of UK Sustainability Indicators, the requirement for a National Annual Environmental Monitoring and Auditing mechanism, reported in the public domain via the Common Inheritance Report series (HMSO,1996) as well as the creation of a number of steering groups e.g. the local Agenda 21 steering group (DoE,1990,1992,1994,1996).

At one level therefore, which we can usefully identify as the administrative or governmental level, UK Agenda 21 actually involves national and local government, a range of steering groups and committees and, because the process is enshrined in legislation, this tier de facto includes the European Union.

The approach operates at a national level in terms of policies, plans and programmes. For example the White Paper (HMSO,1996) makes commitments to sustainable development linked to environmental targets and standards which are relevant to environmental media and environmental resources. In addition the National Environmental Audit has provided a suitable baseline from which such targets and standards can be identified. The UK approach clearly recognises the importance of sustainable development from both a national and international context. However its success in adopting such approaches has been variable. UK Agenda 21 must be viewed in light of existing systems of land management and planning as well as existing systems and approaches to environmental protection.

As, however, in common with the experience in China, programmes and policies based on these principles are still in the process of being introduced. Since the literature is only now beginning to evaluate individual examples of local authority activity, an analysis of outcomes of UK Agenda 21 may thus be premature at other than the level of principle. It would, therefore, be inappropriate here to consider individual examples since, as stated, we are concerned with principles. It should, however, be noted that UK and European practice is sufficiently well advanced to warrant it being offered as a possible template for Agenda 21 developments elsewhere.

From the above it can be seen that the UK Agenda 21 strategy has clearly been built around an existing UK administrative structure in relation to planning and the environment which is itself a manifestation of governmental structure.

In overview then the UK Government can be seen to be actively involved both at a local and central level in the development and application of Agenda 21. The role of the UK national government is as a co-ordination and developer of policy, whilst local government is essentially involved in policy implementation and delivery. Whilst monitoring of achievements is pursued at both levels, central government provides a strong steer on local activities by virtue of its budgetary control of the later.

The Chinese Experience: Sustainability in a Developing Economy

This section provides an overview of what emerges as the key principles in China's Agenda 21. In particular it considers;

- the overarching principles which underpin China's Agenda 21;
- the areas of policy development which will need to be undertaken to secure its stated outcomes;
- the potential to secure an integrated approach to the environment.

Turning first to overarching principles there is evidence to suggest that there is governmental commitment to securing an improvement in China's environmental performance. Clearly the question to be asked is the extent to which Agenda 21 China has been or is in the process of being translated into action. The former Chinese Prime Minister LI Peng in his UN speech on Environment and Development on 12th June 1992 stated:

> We have made environmental protection one of our basic state policies and make unremitting efforts towards this end. In light of our country's actual conditions, we have devised a strategy of synchronised planning, implementation and development in terms of economic development, urban and rural construction, and environmental protection, a strategy that would bring harmony of economic, social and environmental returns. We have improved the legal system in respect of environmental protection and set up relevant organs at various levels and an inter-ministerial co-ordination agency at the national level.

In setting out the factors which support a vision of a strategy of synchronised planning, China's Agenda 21 addresses four distinct but overlapping areas of activity, namely: strategies for sustainable development; sustainability of society; sustainable development of the economy; and protection of resources and the environment.

The key principles of these activities are outlined and the potential for their efficacy is looked at, together with the extent to which administrative structures are in place or are proposed which can support the Agenda 21 process. Examples of policies which emerge from a reading of China Agenda 21 are the intention to develop an integrated transportation system of roads, railways, water and air transport, efforts to be made to protect arable land resources and to limit the amount of arable land used for construction. The pursuit of these clearly illustrate the potential for considerable tension between a pressure for economic development and environmental considerations.

The principal policy instruments which China propose are predicated on scientific data collection and evaluation, legislative, regulatory, managerial and organisational approaches. These are being reinforced by economic measures.

These approaches are succinctly stated in relation to a number of aspects of China Agenda 21. In the context of data collection and analysis, it is stated:

> Action will be taken which will strengthen the foundation for building capacity for sustainable development, in particular by establishing a policy framework for developing social and economic norms for sustainable development, by establishing a system of laws and regulations promoting sustainable development, and by outlining strategic objectives for sustainable development. It will be necessary to establish a comprehensive natural resources and environment monitoring and management system, and to develop planning, statistics and information support systems for social end economic development. It will also be necessary to develop education, raise awareness of sustainable development issues throughout the country and develop domestic capabilities for implementing sustainable development practices.

It is also significant that China Agenda 21 acknowledges that:

> It is particularly necessary that the macro-regulating role of the government for population growth, protection of natural resources and the environment

should be strengthened and that comprehensive decision-making, management and monitoring systems be introduced.

On the issue of legislation it is stated that legislation relating to the economy and sustainable development and legislation concerning the environment and the protection of resources will be introduced. This is particularly significant given that China, unlike the United Kingdom, has the opportunity to legislate in an integrated way. As stated previously the United Kingdom has a very extended history of regulation in the field of environmental control but this has, until recently, tended to deal with a specific aspect of environment, for example legislation addressing aspects of air, water, waste disposal or land use planning have been progressively introduced since the mid 19th century. It is only more recently that UK legislation has responded to the concept of integrated pollution control and linking environmental impact to the development regulation process etc. This has largely been prompted by the policy stance adopted by the European. Given that China is proposing to undertake an ongoing analysis of existing legislation for sustainable development and an examination of legislation related to the environment, resources, energy and industry to determine their completeness and conformity with sustainable development there is a real prospect of introducing more far reaching and holistic legislation from the outset. In addition to the review of national legislation it is also proposed that there will be a scrutiny of local legislation on environmental development to establish compliance between national and local strategies.

In the event that a robust legislative framework is introduced the commitment to require environmental agencies to consider potential impacts on sustainable development when formulating policies and plans is encouraging. It is also highly significant that there is to be new legislation on planning.

It is, however, self evident that legislation of itself cannot achieve an improvement in environmental quality. A major factor in translating the vision of sustainable development and environmental protection into reality is a governmental administrative system which is integrated and flexible in its approach. Indeed we argue that this is a fundamental factor in achieving the aims and objectives of Agenda 21. As with their recognition of the need for a revised legislative framework it is clear that the Chinese government are equally aware of the need, in pursuit of their sustainability objectives, to rationalise and possibly restructure administrative and ministerial portfolios. This is succinctly stated in China Agenda 21 as follows:

China will seek to reform the old system and establish integrated decision making mechanisms tailored to sustainable development. Adjust the functions of existing ministries and agencies and encourage consultation and co-operation amongst ministries and agencies. Establish co-ordinated management and feedback mechanisms so as to co-ordinate actions by different ministries or agencies. As necessary, new organisations will be established to ensure smooth achievement of the strategic goal of sustainable development.'

In the context of economic measures China recognises that:

In order to achieve sustainable economic and social development, China cannot follow the old path of polluting first and cleaning later or damaging first and repairing later, but must rely on full use of economic measures and market mechanisms to promote sustainable development, based on existing conditions and work, simultaneously achieving rapid economic growth, eliminate poverty and protect environment. The establishment of a socialist market economy will serve to help to promote sustainable development.

China Agenda 21 sets out a strategy for the application of taxation and the establishment of an integrated environmental and economic accounting system. In so doing, however, its authors recognise that the present economic development of the country is compromised by its being characterised by its non-rationalised structure, imbalances in regional development, low technological levels and inadequate support mechanisms. The economic strategies which are to be pursued will clearly need the active co-operation of the international community, some of whom are more advanced in developing and applying the systems which China seek to implement.

To compliment legislative, administrative and fiscal measures, China is also looking to secure public participation in their sustainable development strategy. China Agenda 21 acknowledges that the support and participation of public and social groups is essential to achievement of sustainable development.

This is particularly relevant given French's recognition (French,1995) that:

Significantly the Rio conference pointed to the need for a global partnership if sustainable development was to be achieved. One of the requirements for this global partnership is the active participation of citizens in village, municipal, and national political life, as well as the United Nations.

She adds that:

The best hope for improving the process of global governance lies with people and that Agenda 21 encourages the democratisation of international law making by devoting a lengthy section to the important role of major groups (including citizens' groups, labour unions, farmers, women, business interests and others) and by endorsing the need to make information freely and widely available.

At present China Agenda 21 remains a visionary concept and there is little empirical evidence on which to draw to establish its efficacy. If the vision is to be translated into an operative set of policies the proposed legislative framework will need to be supported by an effective administrative system. It is from this perspective that comparative studies may provide a useful benchmark for the parallel development of both legislation and an associated administrative system. The important features to emerge from the analysis of China's Agenda 21 and the country's economic and environmental status are that the need for a sustainability strategy is indispensable and the potential for an integrated environmental management strategy linked to the emerging land use planning system is wholly realistic.

Conclusion

From a consideration of the origins of sustainable development, this chapter started from the proposition that, given the ambiguity which surrounds the concept, little difficulty is experienced by the international community in lending it support and publishing grand schemes for achieving its objectives. In the analysis, however, a mismatch, which may well occur between the published long term vision and its operationalisation, is noted. In addition evidence emerges of the linkages which exist between sustainable development as a visionary concept and the established approach of land use planning. This has more latterly been supplemented by the emerging fields of environmental planning and environmental management albeit they are not yet fully integrated sub-disciplines.

The chapter clearly reviews the significance of China as a rapidly developing economy and its actual and potential environmental impacts at both the national and international levels. It is evident that the exponential growth of the Chinese economy has and is resulting in considerable environmental impacts. These are of significance both within the country in terms of direct costs to industry and government and at an international level, for example in the context of the growth in energy consumption and the attendant contribution to global carbon dioxide mentioned earlier. These underscore the strategic significance of China in the global economy and global environment and lead to the conclusion that the vision expressed in its Agenda 21 must be translated into concrete and effective national policies at the earliest opportunity.

It is clear from the wide ranging policy proposals contained in China's Agenda 21 that they face similar problems in operationalising their vision as do other countries. The example of the United Kingdom's Agenda 21 strategy illustrates the validity of an integrated policy approach to achieving the goals of sustainable development. The chapter also identifies how the historical legacy of the UK's legislative framework and the complexity of its land use planning system has created a number of hurdles. The thrust of the argument is that China, because of the stage it has reached in its economic and legislative development is in a commanding position to introduce an integrated system from the outset. It is also the case that unlike the UK, China's population has not yet become fully divorced from the land and may still retain a rapport with the natural environment.

In the context of an integrated system the developments which have taken place in the land use planning system in the United Kingdom and the extent to which that, in conjunction with a policy of 'integrated pollution control', is now acting as a vehicle for achieving sustainability have been highlighted. The UK's land use planning system has already attracted the attention of the developing world together with those countries who are in the transitional period between a centrally planned economy and a market or socialist market system. In 'exporting' the UK's system of land use planning, we acknowledge that despite the long time scale over which it, and its associated environmental legislation, have developed there remains a discontinuity between the two areas of regulation. More recently there is evidence that in the UK planning and environment are being pursued in a more integrated way. As Lichfield asserts:

> The disciplines of planning and environmental assessment have much to offer each other and yet this has yet to be effectively capitalised upon. Environmental assessment brings to planning an emphasis on systematic analysis (Lichfield,1992).

It is the case that the DoE has attempted to inculcate this as a principle by way of the environmental assessment process (DoE 1996). This is an overt example of the gradual fusion of land use planning, environmental management and environmental planning.

It is worthy of note that the United Kingdom approach has a number of attributes which are not yet clearly identified in the emerging Chinese system. In particular in the UK:

- the land use planning processes place considerable emphasis on public participation but this is as yet little used in the Chinese scenario;
- there is in the UK uniformity of provisions relating to development control in both urban and rural environments and the need to secure planning permission whether within or outside a city boundary but different regimes exist in China between urban and rural areas;
- there is a clearly defined hierarchy and structure to the UK's development control and planning authorities but a more diffuse system in China;
- whilst the UK has adopted a systematic approach to the appraisal of the environmental effects of development plans and proposed developments, this has yet to become a central feature of the Chinese system.

With the above in mind, however, it is not that the UK system merely rests on regulation via its emerging integrated planning system. It is also the case that economic strategies have been introduced to reinforce the regulatory elements, indeed, there is a clear recognition within the United Kingdom's sustainable development strategy that economic instruments and environmental pricing are key factors The UK government's position is that:

> The market is the most effective mechanism for maintaining the momentum of development, sharing its benefits, and for shaping its course towards sustainability; but it cannot give proper weight to environmental considerations unless the costs of environmental damage or the benefits of environmental improvement are built into the prices charged for goods and services. Environmental quality objectives or targets have long played an important part in guiding policies for environmental improvement. Increasingly it will be necessary to develop more specific environmental objectives or targets for different media of the environment or different sectors of the economy as appropriate. The Government is committed to developing instruments which make markets work for the environment and channel development down sustainable paths (HMSO,1994).

Environmental factors belong at the centre of decision making at all levels. Yet to bring them in presents unusual difficulties, and opens up the eventual prospect of radical change in the way society works. In a market economy pricing is a key factor. While recognising that some environmental costs cannot be reckoned in monetary terms, the Panel believes that there should be a greater effort to establish environmental values. There are two broad approaches: through regulation to set and maintain standards, and ensure level competition and some measure of predictability; and through flexible fiscal and economic instruments to provide incentives and disincentives, and ensure that environmental costs are properly taken into account (HMSO,1994).

This position is not, however, universally accepted. Indeed government itself acknowledges that some environmental costs cannot be reckoned in monetary terms. A recognition that economic mechanisms may represent a somewhat blunt approach.

A market led approach is one element in an integrated and dynamic environmental strategy. Environmental management strategies operating via economic incentives may well be limited in terms of, inter alia, pollutant coverage; a recognition that tax when levied in respect of pollutant discharge must be sensitive to the pollutant's damage potential and the benefits derived from its control; and administrative costs may be prohibitive.

It is accepted that these limited comments hardly constitute a critique of market mechanisms, but it is not our intention here to provide such an analysis. These observations merely serve to reinforce the view that market approaches are of themselves only partial, although clearly any meaningful environmental strategy or sustainable development framework will be highly dependent on economic measures. For those unfamiliar with the major economic arguments, Turner provide a starting point for appreciating the issues as well as a bibliographic overview of the more extended literature (Turner,1993).

In conclusion, this chapter is a clear recognition that, whether from the perspective of an advanced market economy or a developing socialist economy, environmental management necessitates international collaboration and effort. It is clear that a UK system of sustainable development, based on regulation via an increasingly integrated environmental management/planning system and reinforced by economic measures, is not immediately transferable to a developing economy and a different cultural perspective. It is, however, suggested that the UK/European experience could act as a stimulus to both the exchange of ideas and the development of a set of internationally recognised criteria against which to evaluate national contributions to global sustainability.

In the context of China, its commitment to legislative, economic and administrative reform points to the need for a mechanism to integrate and co-ordinate national policy. Experience from the United Kingdom supports the view that dealing with environmental issues via a desegregated administrative structure, which seeks to accommodate the range of interested professional, political and business groups, is overly complex. It is evident from the Chinese administrative system that a similar bureaucracy is emerging which may lead to a loss of momentum in achieving China's Agenda 21 objectives. Given the intention to review environmental administrative arrangements, the question needs to be asked whether a co-ordinating body can be identified or formed whose remit is to reconcile competing pressures and to assist in securing both a *sustainable economy* and within a programme of *sustainable development*.

References

Chapter 1

Asian Development Bank (1991), *Asian Development Out Look.*

The Economist Intelligence Unit (1994,1995), *Country Profile: China and Mongolia,* (1993/94, 1994/95), London, UK.

The International Monetary Fund (1993), *'World Economic Outlook'*, the International Herald Tribune.

The United Nations (1991), *World Investment Report on Foreign Direct Investment, the United Nations Centre on Transnational Corporation*, New York.

Overholt, W.H. (1993), *China: the Next Economic Superpower*, Weidenfield and Nicholson, UK.

The State Statistical Bureau of China (1993,1994,1995), *China Statistical Yearbook 1993, 1994, 1995*, the China Statistical Information and Consultancy Service Centre, Beijing, China.

The World Bank (1993,1994,1995), *World Development Report 1993, 1994, 1995*, Oxford University Press, UK.

Chapter 2

The World Bank (1992), *China: Urban Land Management: Options for an Emerging Market Economy*, the World Bank, Washington D.C.

Chapter 3

Chen, J. (1993a), 'The Environment for Direct Investment and the Characteristics of Joint Ventures in China', *Development Policy Review*, Vol.11 No.2, June.

Chen, J. (1993b), 'Social Cost-Benefit Analysis of China's Shenzhen Special Economic Zone', *Development Policy Review*, Vol.11 No.3, September.

Hu, Y. (1993), 'Market Orientated Reforms in China', *Development Policy Review*, Vol.11 No.2, June.

Li, L. (1992), *Land Economy and Management* (in Chinese), China Scientific Press, Beijing, China.

Li, L. (1994), 'Land Policy in the People's Republic of China', *research seminar,* School of Land and Construction Management, University of Greenwich, February.

Walker, A. (1991), *Land, Property and Construction in the People's Republic of China,* Hong Kong University Press, Hong Kong, 1991.

Wall, D. (1993), 'China's Economic Reform and Opening-Up Process: the Special Economic Zones', *Development Policy Review*, Vol.11 No.3, September.

Chapter 4

Cheung, S.N.S. (1994), *'Economic Interactions: China vis-a-vis Hong Kong'*, a university Lecture, The University of Hong Kong, Hong Kong, March.

Hamer, A. (1993), 'Urban China: Looking forward, Looking back', *Proceedings of Conference on Chinese Cities and China's Development,* Centre for Urban Planning and Environmental Management, The University of Hong Kong, Hong Kong.

Kan, F.Y. (1989), 'Reform of Urban Management in China', *Hong Kong Surveyor,* Vol.5, No.1.

Tang, Y. (1989), 'Shenzhen Special Economic Zone, PRC: Property Review', *Hong Kong Surveyor,* Vol.5, No.1.

Walker, A., Chau, K.W. and Lai, L.W.C. (1990), *Hong Kong: Property, Construction and the Economy,* Royal Institution of Chartered Surveyors, London.

Walker, A. (1991), *Land, Property and Construction in the People's Republic of China,* Hong Kong University Press, Hong Kong.

Walker, A. and Flanagan, R. (1991), *Property and Construction in Asian Pacific,* BSP Professional Books, Oxford.

Chapter 5

Abraham-frois, G. and Berrebi, E. (1979), 'Theory of Value', *Prices and Accumulation,* Cambridge University Press.

Brabant, J.M.V. (1987), *Regional Price Formation in Eastern Europe*, Kluwer Academic Publishers.

Hu, C.Z. (1990), 'On the Development, Methodology and Management of Land Value Appraisal System' (in Chinese), *internal report*, the State Land Administration of China, Beijing, China.

Keith, T.J. (1991), 'Applying Discounted Cash Flow Analyses to Land in Transition', *The Appraisal Journal*, October.

Li, L.H. (1995), 'The Official Land Value Appraisal System under the Land Use Rights Reforms in China', *The Appraisal Journal*.

Lichtenstein, P.M. (1983), *An Introduction to Post-Keynesian and Marxian Theories of Value and Price*, New York: M. E. Sharpe Inc.

Lin, Y.Y. (1983), *Valuation of Real Estate* , Taipei: Wen Sheng Publisher (in Chinese).

Needham, Barrie (1992), 'A Theory of Land Prices When Land is Supplied Publicly: The Case of the Netherlands', *Urban Studies*, Vol. 29, No.5.

Marx, K. (1981), *Capital*, Vol.III, Harmondsworth, Middx: Penguin Books in association with New Left Review.

Stigler, G. (1952), 'The Ricardian Theory of Value and Distribution', *Journal of Political Economy*, Vol. 10.

Tang, Y. (1989), 'Urban Land Use in China: Policy Issues and Options', *Land Use Policy*, Vol. 6.

Walker, A. (1991), *Land Property and Construction in the People's Republic of China*, Hong Kong University Press, Hong Kong.

Walker, A. and Li, L.H. (1994), 'Land Use Rights Reform and the Real Estate Market in China', *Journal of Real Estate Literature*, Vol. 2.

Yang C.G. and Liu W.X. (1991), *'Economic Studies on China's Real Estate Market'* (in Chinese), Henan People's Press, Henan, China.

Chapter 6

Chen, J. (1993), 'The Environment for Foreign Direct Investment and the Characteristics of joint ventures in China', *Development Policy Review* Vol. 11, Number 2, Overseas Development Institute, Blackwell Publisher, London, UK.

Harrold, P. and Lall, R. (1993), 'China: Reform and Development in 1992-93', *World Bank Discussion Paper,* No. 215, the World Bank, Washington, D.C., USA.

Lu, Q. (1994), 'The Economic Structure of the PRC Construction Industry', a paper presented at *CIB W55 Annual Meeting*, Hong Kong Polytechnic University, September.

The Economist Intelligence Unit (1994,95), *Country Profile: China and Mongolia*, (1993/94, 1994/95), London, UK.

The State Statistical Bureau of China (1993,1994,1995), China Statistical Yearbook 1993, 1994, 1995, the China Statistical Information and Consultancy Service Centre, Beijing, China.

The World Bank (1993,1994,1995), *World Development Report 1993, 1994, 1995,* Oxford University Press, UK.

Chapter 7

Chan, S. L. (1995), 'An Investigation into the Market Opportunities for Hong Kong Contractors in China and Examination of the Difficulties Encountered', *BSc dissertation*, School of Land and Construction Management, University of Greenwich, UK.

Chen, J. (1993a), 'The Environment for Foreign Direct Investment and the Characteristics of joint ventures in China', *Development Policy Review* Vol. 11, Number 2, Overseas Development Institute, Blackwell Publisher, London, UK.

Chen, J. (1994), 'China: Economic Growth and Construction Activity', Strategic Planning in Construction Companies', *A. J. Etkin International Seminar on Strategic Planning in Construction Companies*, Technion, Haifa, Israel.

The Department of Environment (1994), *Second Report on Opportunities for UK Construction Companies in China*, prepared by He J., HMSO, London.

The Department of Environment (1995), *Fourth Report on Opportunities for UK Construction Companies in China*, prepared by He J., HMSO, London.

The Economist Intelligence Unit (1994), *Country Profile: China and Mongolia*, (1993/94), London, UK.

The State Statistical Bureau of China (1993), *China Statistical Yearbook 1993*, the China Statistical Information and Consultancy Service Centre, Beijing, China.

Wills, D. (1992), 'Construction Opportunities in Asia Pacific Rim', *International Construction Management Forum*, London.

Yen, S. R. (1985), 'Why the Construction Market in China is Unique', *China Construction 85'*, Institute of International Research, Hong Kong, June.

Chapter 8

Chen, J. (1991), *Foreign Direct Investment in China: Policies and Performance*, PhD thesis, Lancaster University, UK.

Chen, J. (1993b), 'Social Cost-Benefit Analysis of China's Shenzhen Special Economic Zone', *Development Policy Review* Vol. 11, Number 3, Overseas Development Institute, Blackwell Publisher, London, UK.

Chen, J. (1994), 'China: Economic Growth and Construction Activity', Strategic Planning in Construction Companies, A. J. Etkin *International Seminar on Strategic Planning in Construction Companies*, Technion, Haifa, Israel.

The Economist Intelligence Unit (1993): *Country Profile: China and Mongolia*, (1993/94), London, UK.

Little, I.M.D. and Mirlees, J.A. (1974), *Project Appraisal and Planning for Developing Countries*, Heinemann Educational Books Ltd., London.

Oborne, M. (1986), *China's Special Economic Zones*, Development Centre of the Organisation for Economic Co-operation and Development, OECD, Paris.

The State Statistical Bureau of China (1993), *China Statistical Yearbook 1993*, the China Statistical Information and Consultancy Service Centre, Beijing, China.

Warr, P.G. (1986), 'Export Promotion via Industrial Enclaves - The Philippines' Bataan Export Processing Zone', *Working paper*, Department of Economics, Research School of Pacific Studies, Australian National University.

Chapter 9

Barlow, M. (1988), *'Urban Housing Reforms in China: A First Overview'*, Working on Urban Development Division of the Policy, Planning and Research Department, World Bank, Washington D.C.

The Economist (1995), 'China's State Enterprises', *The Economist*, June 10th-16th 1995, Vol.335, No.7918, UK.

The Department of Environment (1994), *Second Report on Opportunities for UK Construction Companies in China,* prepared by He J., HMSO, London.

The Department of Environment (1995), *Fourth Report on Opportunities for UK Construction Companies in China,* prepared by He J., HMSO, London.

Wang, Y. (1989), *'Housing Commercialisation and Inflation'*, The State Council of China.

Chapter 10

Blowers, A. (1992), 'Planing a Sustainable Future: Problems, Principles and Prospects', *Town and Country Planning.* Volume 61 No 5.

Chen, D. (1991), 'Problems and Suggestions of Chinese Agriculture Development', *People's Daily* (Overseas Edition), 10th January.

Council for the Protection of Rural England (1995), *Towards Sustainability,* London.

China's Science News Agency (1989), 'Saving and Development', *internal report printed by the Chinese Academy of Science,* Beijing.

Department of the Environment (1990), *This Common Inheritance,* HMSO, London.

Department of the Environment (1992), *The Functions of Local Authorities in Britain,* HMSO, London.

Department of the Environment (1996), *Indicators of Sustainable Development in the United Kingdom,* HMSO, London.

Dwyer, D. (1994), *China: The Next Decades,* Longman Scientific & Technical, UK.

The Economist Intelligence Unit Limited (1995), County Forecast: China, 4th Quarter, London, UK.

Florig, K.H. (1993), 'Benefits of Air Pollution Reduction in China', Mimeo, prepared *Sustainable Development: The UK Strategy,* HMSO.

French, H. (1995), 'Forging a New Global Partnership', *Strategic World Report,* World Watch Institute.

Friends of the Earth (1994), *Planing for the Planet,* London.

Hajer, M.A. (1996), 'Ecological Modernisation as Cultural Politics', in Lash, S. (eds.), *Risk, Environment and Modernity,* Sage, London.

HMSO (1994), *Sustainable Development: The UK Strategy,* London.

HMSO (1995), *The Government of Britain,* London.

HMSO (1996), *This Common Inheritance: UK Annual Report*, London.

Local Agenda 21 Steering Group (1994), *Taking Rio Forward*, London.

(Lees,1991) Lees, R.M., 'China and the World in the Nineties', summary report of the *International Conference on Economic Development and Environment in China*, 25th January.

Lichfield, N. (1992), 'The Integration of Environmental Assessment into Development Planning: Part 1 Some Principles', *Project Appraisal*, Vol 7 No 2.

Lichfield, N. (1992), 'The Integration of Environmental Assessment into Development Planning: Part 2 Some Principles', *Project Appraisal*, Vol 7 No 3.

Lucas, K., and Chambers, D. (1996), 'Towards a Deconstruction of Environment in the Thames Gateway', *Policy Studies*, London.

Ministry of Public Health, P.R. China (1988), *Health Statistics in China 1988*, Beijing, China.

Organisation for Economic Co-operation and Development (1995), *Planning for Sustainable Development. Country Experiences*, Paris.

Palmer, C. (1994), 'Some Problems with Sustainability Studies', *Christian Ethics*, Vol 2.

Pearce, D. (1993), Blueprint for a Green Economy, *Earthscan*, London.

Polenske, K.R. and Lin, X. (1993) 'Conserving Energy to Reduce Carbon Dioxide Emissions in China', *Structural Change and Economic Dynamics*, Vol.4, No.2.

Redclift, M. (1993), 'Sustainable Development: Needs, Values', *Rights. Environmental Values*. 2 Vol 1, Spring.

Roberts, P. (1996), 'Ecological Modernisation Approaches to Regional and Urban Planning and Development', *International Conference on Environment Planning and Land Use*, Keele University, UK, April.

Ryan, M. and Flavin, C. (1995), 'Facing China's Limits', *State of the World Report*, World Watch Institute, Washington, USA, 1995.

Rydin, Y. (1993), The British Planning System, Macmillan Press, 1993.

State Environmental Protection Commission and State Planning Commission (1994), '*Internal Report on Environmental Protection*'.

Sinton, J.E. and Mark, D.L. (1994), 'Changing Energy Intensity in Chinese Industry: The Relative Importance of Structural Shift and Intensity Change', *Energy Policy*, Vol.22, No.3, March.

The State Statistical Bureau of China (1992,1993,1994,1995), *China Statistical Yearbook* 1992, 1993, 1994, 1995, the China Statistical Information and Consultancy Service Centre, Beijing.

Turner, R.K., Pearce, D. and Bateman, I. (1994), *Environmental Economics,* Harvester Wheatsheaf.

The United Nations (1994), World Economic Survey 1994, UN, New York.

The United Nations (1992), *United Nations Conference on Environment and Development,* proceedings published by UN.

Wang, J. (1989), 'Water Pollution and Water Shortage Problems in China', *Journal of Applied Ecology,* Vol. 26.

The World Bank (1992a), China: *Environmental Strategy Paper,* Vol.1, Washington, D.C., USA.

The World Bank (1992b), *World Development Report 1992,* Washington D.C., USA.

The World Bank (1995), *World Development Report 1995,* Washington D.C., USA.

Zhao, Y. and Doung, Y. (1990), 'On the Discussion of the Water Pollution Control and Eco-environment Construction in Small Size Cities and Towns of China', *Rural Ecological Environment,* Vol.21, 1990.

British Government Panel (1995), *British Government Panel on Sustainable Development,* First Report, January.

British Government Panel (1996), British Government Panel on sustainable Development, Second Report, January.

Chinese Government (1994), *China's Agenda 21,* China Environmental Science Press.

Local Government (1996), 'Report on China's Urban Health Programme', Yuzhong District, Chongqing, China, March.

European Commission (1992), "Towards Sustainability", *A European Programme of Policy and Action in Relation to the Environment and Sustainable Development COM (92),* 23 Final Vol 11, Brussels. March.

*For Product Safety Concerns and Information please contact
our EU representative GPSR@taylorandfrancis.com Taylor & Francis
Verlag GmbH, Kaufingerstraße 24, 80331 München, Germany*

T - #0033 - 230425 - C0 - 215/145/10 [12] - CB - 9781138343665 - Gloss Lamination